Mark and the Elijah-Elisha Narrative

Mark and the Elijah-Elisha Narrative

*Considering the Practice of Greco-Roman Imitation
in the Search for Markan Source Material*

ADAM WINN

☙PICKWICK *Publications* • Eugene, Oregon

MARK AND THE ELIJAH-ELISHA NARRATIVE
Considering the Practice of Greco-Roman Imitation
in the Search for Markan Source Material

Copyright © 2010 Adam Winn. All rights reserved. Except for brief quotations in critical publications or reviews, no part of this book may be reproduced in any manner without prior written permission from the publisher. Write: Permissions, Wipf and Stock Publishers, 199 W. 8th Ave., Suite 3, Eugene, OR 97401.

Pickwick Publications
An Imprint of Wipf and Stock Publishers
199 W. 8th Ave., Suite 3
Eugene, OR 97401

www.wipfandstock.com

ISBN 13: 978-1-60899-201-0

Cataloging-in-Publication data:

Winn, Adam.

Mark and the Elijah-Elisha narrative : considering the practice of Greco-Roman imitation in the search for Markan source material / Adam Winn.

xii + 136 p.; 23 cm. Includes bibliographical references and indexes.

ISBN 13: 978-1-60899-201-0

1. Bible. N.T. Mark—Criticism, interpretation, etc. 2. Bible. N.T. Mark—Relation to Kings. 3. Elijah (Biblical prophets). 4. Elisha (Biblical prophets). I. Title

BS2585.52.W56 2010

Manufactured in the U.S.A.

*To Brennan Grace Winn, my daughter
and little princess who brightens my every day*

Contents

Acknowledgments / ix

Preliminary Remarks and Abbreviations / xi

Introduction / 1

1　The Imitation of Homer's *Iliad* and *Odyssey* in Virgil's *Aeneid* / 11

2　Mark and Imitation / 34

3　Mark and the Elijah-Elisha Narrative / 51

4　General Similarities between Mark and the Elijah-Elisha Narrative / 61

5　Mark 1:1–20 and the Elijah-Elisha Narrative / 69

6　Mark's Galilean Ministry and the Elijah-Elisha Narrative / 77

7　Mark's Passion Predictions and the Elijah-Elisha Narrative / 92

8　The Parable of the Wicked Tenants and the Elijah-Elisha Narrative / 100

9　Mark's Passion and Resurrection Narratives and the Elijah-Elisha Narrative / 109

Conclusions / 117

Bibliography / 121

Subject Index / 129

Author Index / 131

Ancient Literature Index / 133

Acknowledgments

THIS BOOK IS THE fruit of a Postdoctoral Research Fellowship done at the Dominican Biblical Institute (DBI) in Limerick, Ireland during the 2008–2009 academic year. This fellowship proved to be a tremendous blessing to my family and me, and it is only fitting to offer words of thanks to those who made it so.

First and foremost, I must thank Thomas Brodie, who granted me the fellowship and supervised my research and writing. His erudition, careful guidance, and flexibility were greatly appreciated and integral to this project's success. Yet equally appreciated were his collegiality, sense of humor, and friendship—all of which provided for a warm and enjoyable setting for research. Tom, your love and support to myself and my family mean more than words could say. You were truly a father to us.

Many thanks are also due to two additional DBI employees, Margaret (Peig) McGrath and Brendan Clifford, both of whom helped tremdously with our relocation to and life in Ireland. Without Peig, who helped us with everything from setting up a bank account to properly preparing morning tea, I wonder how we would ever have survived. Brendan was the first one to greet us when we arrived in Ireland. Throughout our stay, his many acts of service and his kind words and manner blessed our family greatly.

I must thank the DBI's board of directors who approved the research fellowship that I received. Your sincere support of both myself as well as the DBI is greatly appreciated. The DBI is doing great work, and you help make that possible.

I offer sincere thanks to my fellow research colleagues at the DBI: Tom Nelligan, John Shelton, and Il-Seung Chung (as well as their families). Your willingness to discuss, review, and critique my work was invaluable, and certainly strengthened the final product a great deal. More significant however, was your encouragement, support, humor, and friendship that brought true joy to our family's stay in Ireland.

Acknowledgments

    I thank the Irish people and all the friends we made during our time on the Emerald Isle. We were welcomed to your beautiful country with open arms, and you made your country feel like our home.

    I thank the people at Wipf and Stock Publishing, in particular Dr. K. C. Hanson, Dr. Chris Spinks, and Christian Amondson, not only for accepting this project for publication, but also for their excellence and professionalism in its production. It has been a pleasure working with all of you.

    I thank both my parents and my in-laws, who not only regularly sent us care packages with "treats" from the states but also made our traveling to and from Ireland finacially feasible. As always, your love and support accompanies all we do!

    I thank my family—my wife Molly and my daughter Brennan. Brennan, thank you for enduring such long trips to and from Ireland with your mommy and daddy—for a two-year-old, those trips were quite an accomplishment! You brought joy to every day we spent in Ireland, and I hope one day you can return to that beautiful country. Molly, I thank you for your willingness to go on this adventure with me. While it was not always easy or convenient, it allowed us to create memories of each other and our family that we will share for a lifetime. I look forward to the rest of our adventures together, and I will love you through them all.

    Finally, I must thank the God and Father my Lord Jesus Christ, without whom we would have none of the above to be thankful for. For all the blessings and successes in my life, including the success of this book, I give Him all honor, glory, and praise. Amen.

Preliminary Remarks and Abbreviations

ALL CITATIONS FROM THE Old and New Testament come from the New Revised Standard Version unless otherwise noted. Any Greek texts from the New Testament are taken from the Nestle-Aland 27th edition. Greek and Latin texts from ancient authors are taken from the Loeb Classical Library unless otherwise noted.

The abbreviations used in this book follow those provided in *The SBL Handbook of Style for Ancient Near Eastern, Biblical, and Early Christian Studies* (edited by P. H. Alexander et al., Peabody, MA: Hendrickson, 1999). These abbreviations include those for academic journals, commentary and monograph series, biblical books and other ancient literature.

Introduction

MARKAN SOURCES: THE CURRENT STATE OF RESEARCH

THE AMOUNT OF SCHOLARSHIP put forth for the interpretation of Mark's gospel in the past century is enormous, with more new Markan scholarship being produced every year. Yet in light of this vast amount of secondary literature on Mark, the dearth of scholarship devoted to Markan literary sources is striking.[1] This absence is all the more remarkable given the attention paid to source material in the study of the other three canonical gospels. One cannot pick a modern commentary on Luke or Matthew (and to some degree John) and not find a discussion on the source material for these literary works. But in a survey of commentaries on Mark, only three could be found that offer a discussion of Markan source material. Of these three, only one discussed Mark's use of extant texts—that of C. S. Mann, a proponent of the "Griesbach Hypothesis," discusses Mark's use of Matthew and Luke.[2] The other two commentaries only discuss "pre-Markan" or oral traditions, but offer no discussion on Mark's use of extant texts as source material.[3] In fact, only three significant studies could be found that seriously consider extant texts as possible source material for Mark's gospel.[4]

---

1. Clearly many Markan interpreters have recognized and analyzed Mark's use of Jewish Scriptures (e.g., the evangelist's direct quotation of scripture, obvious allusions to scripture, or faint echoes of scripture). While such scholarly efforts are valuable for Markan exegesis and technically do consider Mark's use of extant literature, they are not, as a general rule, considering Jewish Scriptures as a substantial source for Mark's narrative content, themes, details, and/or structure. It might be best to say that while many Markan interpreters have considered literary influences on Mark's gospel, few have considered the literary sources for Mark's gospel.

2. See Mann, *Mark*.

3. See Guelich, *Mark 1—8:26*, 57–58; Marcus, *Mark 1–8*. It should be noted that Marcus does discuss similarities between Mark and Paul, but does not go as far as suggesting a literary relationship between them.

4. See MacDonald, *Homeric Epics*; Brodie, *Crucial Bridge*, 86–95. This section has

Why is there such an absence of scholarly consideration of Mark's use of extant texts? We suggest that the reason is directly related to the limited paradigm that New Testament scholarship has inherited from source, form, and redaction criticism. Source criticism, intentionally or unintentionally, limited the sphere of possible gospel sources to like-texts. It was presumed that for a text to be the source of gospel, it had to a gospel itself, or be quite close to one. All theories in the complicated quest for a solution to the synoptic problem operated on this assumption. Hypothetical texts such as "Urmarkus" and "Proto-Luke" were gospels.[5] Even Q, as much as some interpreters might champion its distinction from our canonical gospels and its identity as a sayings source, includes teachings, parables, and actions of Jesus. Though it may not have a distinct narrative structure, Q is still a collection of Jesus traditions that is similar to the canonical gospels in more ways than it is not. Therefore, given this limited scope in what is a possible source for a gospel, the establishment of Markan priority by source criticism closed the door on the search for Markan sources. If sources for gospels can only be gospel-like material, and Mark is the first gospel, then no avenue exists for uncovering Markan literary sources. We are simply left to conclude that Mark is a unique and original creation—one that is independent of significant literary sources.

If source criticism shut the door on the search for Markan literary sources, form criticism locked it by proposing that the sources for Mark's gospel were in fact not literary at all, but oral. The Markan evangelist simply compiled oral traditions from the early church and strung them together to form a rough narrative.[6] Presumably, the Markan evangelist (or compiler) did not use any extant literature as primary source material. Form criticism gave the definitive answer to the question of Markan sources, and sadly, this answer was left virtually unchallenged by gospel

---

been republished as a chapter in Brodie's more recent work, *Birthing*, 147–53; Roth, *Hebrew Gospel*.

5. On "Proto-Luke," see Feine, *Eine vorkanonische Überlieferung des Lukas*; Streeter, *The Four Gospels*, 2–32, 182–215; Sahlin, *Der Messias und das Gottesfolk*. For a brief but helpful discussion on the history of Proto-Luke, see Brodie, *Birthing*, 541–44. For interpreters who proposed an "Urmarkus," see Weizsacker, *Untersuchungen über die evangelische Geschichte*; Holtzmann, *Die synoptischen Evangelien*; Moffatt, *An Introduction to the Literature of the New Testament*; Feine, *Einleitung in das Neue Testament*.

6. For examples of New Testament form critics, see Bultmann, *Synoptic Tradition*; Dibelius, *Tradition to Gospel*; and Taylor, *Gospel Tradition*. For information on form criticism and the New Testament, see Blomberg, "Form Criticism," 243–50; and Robbins, "Form Criticism."

Introduction

interpreters. In fact, today this assumption of form criticism still dominates virtually all current scholarly discussion of Mark's origin and formation. With this presumption that the sources for the first gospel were oral, naturally there has been little effort to discern any possible literary sources the first gospel may have used.

After source criticism shut the door on the search for Markan literary sources and form criticism locked it, redaction criticism essentially threw away the key, leaving the door permanently shut. As redaction critics sought to determine when and how one gospel writer was editing the work of another, they established, at least in practice, stringent criteria for determining literary dependence. Generally, two things seem to be required to demonstrate literary dependence: (1) specific agreement in details/order; and (2) strong verbal agreement. With these strict standards for determining literary dependence, any scholar who, in the face of source and form criticism, seeks to establish literary sources for Mark's gospel faces the near impossible task of doing so.

Here we will give two examples to demonstrate not only the pride of place gospel scholars give to verbal agreement and specific agreement of order/detail in determining literary dependence, but also the difficulty one might face in proving Mark's dependence on a non-gospel source. Our first example, will be the Johannine account of Jesus healing an official's son (John 4:46–54). This story is closely paralleled by the Matthean and Lukan account of Jesus healing the son/servant of a Roman centurion (Matt 8:15–13//Luke 7:1–10). The similar details of the two stories can bee seen in the chart below.

Matt 8:5–13/Luke 7:1–10	John 4:46–54
Story takes place in Capernaum	Story takes place in Capernaum
Story involves a person of rank (Centurion)	Story involves a person of rank (Official)
Story involves a sick boy (son/servant)	Story involves a sick boy (son)
A request for healing is made	A request for healing is made
Jesus heals the boy from a great distance	Jesus heals the boy from a great distance
The healing takes place at the moment of Jesus' promise of healing (in Matt. only)	The healing takes place at the moment of Jesus' promise of healing
Faith/belief plays a prominent role in the story	Faith/belief plays a prominent role in the story

3

The parallels between these stories are striking, and in fact they lead most interpreters to conclude that all three gospels are reflecting the same story/tradition. However, because the stories have little verbal agreement and lack specificity in the agreement of certain details, many interpreters conclude that John's account of the story is independent of both Matthew's and Luke's account.[7] Although the stories may share a common tradition (likely an oral one!), any literary relationship between John and either of the synoptic accounts is generally rejected.

Another noteworthy example is the four different accounts of the words of institution at the last supper (Matt 26:26–29; Mark 14:22–25; Luke 22:15–20; 1 Cor 11:23–25). Below, all four texts are presented in parallel columns.

---

7. For examples of interpreters who make such conclusions, see Brown, *Gospel according to John*, 192–93; Dodd, *Historical Tradition in the Fourth Gospel*; Schnackenburg, *St. John*, 1:471–75; Haenchen, *John*, 236–37; Morris, *The Gospel according to John*, 254–56; Beasley-Murray, *John*, 71. One noteworthy exception to this trend in Johannine scholarship is the conclusion of C. K. Barrett, who concludes that John is directly dependent upon the synoptics. Interestingly enough, his decision is largely based on a handful of verbal agreements! See Barrett, *Gospel according to St. John*, 245.

Introduction

Matthew 26:26–29	Mark 14:22–25	Luke 22:15–20	1 Corinthians 11:23–25
Εσθιόντων δὲ **αὐτῶν λαβὼν** ὁ Ἰησοῦς **ἄρτον** καὶ **εὐλογήσας ἔκλασεν** καὶ **δοὺς** τοῖς μαθηταῖς **εἶπεν**– **λάβετε** φάγετε, **τοῦτό ἐστιν τὸ σῶμά μου.** ²⁷ **καὶ λαβὼν ποτήριον** καὶ **εὐχαριστήσας ἔδωκεν αὐτοῖς** λέγων• **πίετε ἐξ αὐτοῦ πάντες,** ²⁸ **τοῦτο** γάρ **ἐστιν τὸ αἷμά μου τῆς διαθήκης** τὸ περὶ πολλῶν **ἐκχυννόμενον** εἰς ἄφεσιν ἁμαρτιῶν. ²⁹ λέγω δὲ ὑμῖν, οὐ μὴ πίω ἀπ' ἄρτι ἐκ τούτου **τοῦ γενήματος τῆς ἀμπέλου ἕως τῆς ἡμέρας ἐκείνης ὅταν αὐτὸ πίνω** μεθ' ὑμῶν **καινὸν ἐν τῇ βασιλείᾳ** τοῦ πατρός μου.	Καὶ **ἐσθιόντων αὐτῶν λαβὼν ἄρτον εὐλογήσας ἔκλασεν καὶ ἔδωκεν αὐτοῖς καὶ εἶπεν• λάβετε, τοῦτό ἐστιν τὸ σῶμά μου.** ²³ **καὶ λαβὼν ποτήριον εὐχαριστήσας ἔδωκεν αὐτοῖς, καὶ ἔπιον ἐξ αὐτοῦ πάντες.** ²⁴ **καὶ εἶπεν αὐτοῖς• τοῦτό ἐστιν τὸ αἷμά μου τῆς διαθήκης τὸ ἐκχυννόμενον ὑπὲρ πολλῶν.** ²⁵ ἀμὴν λέγω ὑμῖν ὅτι οὐκέτι **οὐ μὴ πίω ἐκ τοῦ γενήματος τῆς ἀμπέλου ἕως τῆς ἡμέρας ἐκείνης ὅταν αὐτὸ πίνω καινὸν ἐν τῇ βασιλείᾳ** τοῦ θεοῦ.	καὶ εἶπεν πρὸς αὐτούς• ἐπιθυμίᾳ ἐπεθύμησα τοῦτο τὸ πάσχα φαγεῖν μεθ' ὑμῶν πρὸ τοῦ με παθεῖν• ¹⁶ λέγω γὰρ ὑμῖν ὅτι οὐ μὴ φάγω αὐτὸ ἕως ὅτου πληρωθῇ **ἐν τῇ βασιλείᾳ τοῦ θεοῦ.** ¹⁷ καὶ δεξάμενος **ποτήριον εὐχαριστήσας** εἶπεν• λάβετε τοῦτο καὶ διαμερίσατε εἰς ἑαυτούς• ¹⁸ λέγω γὰρ ὑμῖν, [ὅτι] **οὐ μὴ πίω** ἀπὸ τοῦ νῦν ἀπὸ **τοῦ γενήματος τῆς ἀμπέλου ἕως** οὗ ἡ **βασιλεία τοῦ θεοῦ** ἔλθη. ¹⁹ καὶ **λαβὼν ἄρτον εὐχαριστήσας** ἔκλασεν **καὶ ἔδωκεν αὐτοῖς** λέγων• **τοῦτό ἐστιν τὸ σῶμά μου** <u>τὸ ὑπὲρ ὑμῶν διδόμενον• τοῦτο ποιεῖτε εἰς τὴν ἐμὴν ἀνάμνησιν.</u> ²⁰ καὶ **τὸ ποτήριον** <u>ὡσαύτως μετὰ τὸ δειπνῆσαι, λέγων• τοῦτο τὸ ποτήριον ἡ καινὴ διαθήκη ἐν τῷ αἵματί μου τὸ</u> **ὑπὲρ** ὑμῶν **ἐκχυννόμενον.**	Ἐγὼ γὰρ παρέλαβον ἀπὸ τοῦ κυρίου, ὃ καὶ παρέδωκα ὑμῖν, ὅτι ὁ κύριος Ἰησοῦς ἐν τῇ νυκτὶ ᾗ παρεδίδετο **ἔλαβεν ἄρτον** ²⁴ καὶ **εὐχαριστήσας** ἔκλασεν καὶ εἶπεν• **τοῦτό μού ἐστιν τὸ σῶμα** <u>τὸ ὑπὲρ ὑμῶν• τοῦτο ποιεῖτε εἰς τὴν ἐμὴν ἀνάμνησιν.</u> <u>²⁵ ὡσαύτως</u> καὶ τὸ **ποτήριον** <u>μετὰ τὸ δειπνῆσαι λέγων• τοῦτο τὸ ποτήριον ἡ</u> **καινὴ διαθήκη ἐστὶν** <u>ἐν τῷ ἐμῷ αἵματι•</u> τοῦτο ποιεῖτε, ὁσάκις ἐὰν πίνητε, εἰς τὴν ἐμὴν ἀνάμνησιν.

Matthew 26:26–29	Mark 14:22–25	Luke 22:15–20	1 Corinthians 11:23–25
(NRSV) **While they were eating, Jesus took a loaf of bread, and after blessing it he broke it, gave it** to the disciples, **and said, "Take, eat; this is my body."** [27] **Then he took a cup, and after giving thanks he gave it to them,** saying, **"Drink from it, all of you;** [28] for **this is my blood of the covenant, which is poured out for many** for the forgiveness of sins. [29] **I tell you, I will never again drink of this fruit of the vine until that day when I drink it new with you in my** Father's **kingdom."**	(NRSV) **While they were eating, he took a loaf of bread, and after blessing it he broke it, gave it** to them, **and said, "Take; this is my body."** [23] **Then he took a cup, and after giving thanks he gave it to them,** and all of **them drank from it.** [24] He said to them, **"This is my blood of the covenant, which is poured out for many.** [25] Truly **I tell you, I will never again drink of the fruit of the vine until that day when I drink it new in the kingdom of God."**	(NRSV) He said to them, "I have eagerly desired to eat this Passover with you before I suffer; [16] for I tell you, I will not eat it **until it is fulfilled in the kingdom of God."** [17] **Then he took a cup, and after giving thanks** he said, "Take this and divide it among yourselves; [18] for I tell you that from now on **I will not drink of the fruit of the vine until the kingdom** of God comes." [19] Then he took a loaf of bread, and when he **had given thanks, he broke it and gave it to them,** saying, **"This is my body,** *which is given for you. Do this in remembrance of me."* [20] And he did the *same* with the *cup after supper,* saying, "This cup that **is poured out** for you *is the new covenant in my blood.*	(NRSV) For I received from the Lord what I also handed on to you, that the Lord Jesus on the night when he was betrayed took a loaf of bread, [24] and when he had given thanks, **he broke it** and said, **"This is my body** *that is for you. Do this in remembrance of me."* [25] In the same way he took the *cup also, after supper, saying, "This cup is the new covenant in my blood.* Do this, as often as you drink it, in remembrance of me."

While there are some minor differences between these four passages, they are strikingly similar in many ways, even with regard to their verbal agreement. But it is generally concluded that these four sayings represent two independent traditions, with Matthew and Mark representing one

Introduction

tradition and Luke and 1 Corinthians representing another.[8] Again, the minor differences in detail and the lack of strong verbal agreement seem to preclude the possibility that three of these traditions might all ultimately be dependent on the earliest one.

Therefore, source criticism made the search for Markan literary sources irrelevant through the establishment of Markan priority. Form criticism removed the need for the search altogether by promoting oral traditions over literary ones. Finally, redaction criticism provided such strict standards for literary dependence that anyone who still might be interested in the search for Markan sources would find it next to impossible. In light of these three influences, it is no wonder that virtually no attempts have been made by Markan interpreters to find literary sources for the first gospel.

CRITIQUING THE CURRENT STATE OF RESEARCH

Here we argue that the search for Markan sources is being restrained unnecessarily by faulty presuppositions and criteria. First, simply because Mark's gospel is regarded as the first narrative account of the life of Jesus does not mean that it was not without literary precedence or that Mark was not dependent on literary sources. Our knowledge that ancient writing was an imitative art argues against the conclusion that gospel sources must be other gospels. The gospel writers had an abundant number of literary sources from which to construct their narratives (e.g., Jewish Scripture, Greco-Roman epics, etc.). The presupposition that Mark's gospel relied primarily, if not exclusively, on oral tradition is greatly misguided and again is undermined by our knowledge of ancient writing practices.[9] We are not claiming that oral traditions did not influence the formation of Mark's gospel, but we are claiming that literary influences were at least equally influential on the gospel's formation.[10] It is therefore of great importance that the question of Mark's literary sources be reopened. If these sources could be determined—even to a minor degree—the interpretive pay off would be significant, shedding light on a vast number of Markan

8. For example, see Stein, "Last Supper," 445; O'Toole, "Last Supper," 237–39.

9. See Brodie's critique of the theory of oral tradition in the formation of the gospels; *Birthing*, 50–62.

10. A full-blown critique of oral tradition is not our intention here. We only seek to reject the wide spread assumption that Mark's sources were primarily (or only) oral rather than literary.

interpretive issues. The topic of Markan sources is far from irrelevant, and should be considered a pressing issue for any Markan interpreter.

Second, the process of detecting Markan sources or Markan literary dependence on other texts is far from impossible. The strict criteria used by redaction critics (and most contemporary gospel interpreters) in determining literary dependence are too restricting, and need to be significantly revised in light of ancient writing practices—in particular the practice of *mimesis* or *imitatio*. While strong verbal agreement and specific similarity in detail are certainly strong criteria for determining literary dependence, they are far from the only criteria, and their absence does not and should not automatically preclude such dependence. Any search for Markan sources will require the development of sound criteria for establishing literary dependence, but such development is possible, making the search for Markan literary sources equally possible.

A WAY FORWARD IN THE SEARCH FOR MARKAN SOURCES

Recently, a number of publications in the field of gospel studies have shed light on the practice of *mimesis* or imitation in the ancient literary world.[11] Contra the modern literary world, which is obsessed with originality and both new and inventive content, the ancient world was obsessed with imitating the great works (oratory, literary, sculpture, etc.) that were already in existence.[12] Isocrates strongly stressed the need for students to imitate their teacher.[13] Cicero states "Let this then be my first counsel, that we show the student [of rhetoric] whom to copy."[14] (Cicero, *On the Orator* 2.21.90, Sutton and Rackham, LCL). Quintillian regarded repeated reading of great works as a necessary step in the process of imitation.[15]

---

11. See MacDonald, *Homeric Epics*, esp. 1–14; Brodie, *Birthing*, esp. 3–22; O'Leary, *Matthew's Judaization of Mark*, esp. 9–24.

12. This concept of imitation is not only found in the world of ancient literature, but can be seen in art and philosophy as well. For Plato, the entire world was simply an imitation of ideal heavenly forms and for Aristotle, all art was an imitation of nature. For discussion on Plato and imitation, see McKeon, "Imitation," 3–16; Plato *Republic* 3.392D–394C; 4.500C–E. For discussion on Aristotle and imitation, see McKeon, "Imitation," 16–26; Aristotle *Physics* 2.2.194a22; 2.8.199a15–17.

13. Isocrates *Soph.* 17–18; *Paneg.* 10.

14. Cicero *De or.* 2.21.90.

15. Quintillian, *Inst.* 10.1.19–20.

Introduction

Examples of ancient imitation are abundant in the Greco-Roman world; its ubiquity in ancient literature is impossible to deny.[16]

Through the study of imitation in ancient Greco-Roman literature, we have a rare and significant window into the way in which ancient authors used literary sources. The access to such a window makes it all the more striking how small a role the concept and practice of *mimesis*/imitation has played in the field of gospel studies—a field that is dominated with necessary concerns about the origin of texts, intertextuality, and literary sources. In exploring these issues, gospel interpreters have virtually ignored perhaps the greatest window we have into the way ancient authors used literary texts in their compositions. Certainly by studying the way in which ancient authors imitated and rewrote extant sources, we can gain insights into how the gospel authors might have used each other or even other extant literature to compose gospels. In fact, we might even be able to better detect the sources that particular author's might have used, if through the study of imitation, we could develop criteria for determining literary dependence.

Therefore, the study of imitation gives us a way forward in our search for Markan sources. By examining the typical ways in which ancient authors imitated other texts, we will have a window into how the Markan evangelist might have used other texts. We also ought to be able to develop new criteria—beyond that which has been used by redaction critics—for determining whether literary dependence exists between Mark and other extant literature.

MOVING FORWARD: THE PURPOSE AND OUTLINE OF THE PRESENT STUDY

Until now, only two people have seriously used *mimesis*/imitation as a way of identifying Markan sources. The first and perhaps most recognized attempt is that of Dennis MacDonald who argues for Markan imitation of Homer's *Iliad* and *Odyssey*.[17] MacDonald begins his study discussing the concept and practice of *mimesis* in the ancient world, and offers criteria for determining literary dependence. Throughout the rest of the book, MacDonald seeks to demonstrate Mark's literary dependence on Homer.

---

16. For discussion and bibliography on ancient authors who practiced imitation/*mimesis*, see Nelis, *Virgil's Aeneid*, 12–13, esp. 13 n. 56.

17. MacDonald, *Homeric Epics*.

The second attempt to use *mimesis* to identify Markan sources is that of Thomas L. Brodie who suggests Markan imitation of the Septuagintal Elijah-Elisha narrative in 1 and 2 Kings.[18] Brodie's work is, by his own admission, preliminary and cursory, and requiring further investigation of the topic. Yet, Brodie has laid important ground work for such an investigation, noting numerous and striking parallels between Mark's gospel and the Elijah-Elisha narrative.

The purpose of the present project is to build on the preliminary work already done by Brodie, and explore the possibility that Mark's gospel is imitating the Elijah-Elisha narrative. However, the project will begin by further exploring the process of imitation and rewriting in the ancient world. The first chapter will analyze the way in which Virgil imitated Homer's *Iliad* and *Odyssey* in his *Aeneid*. The analysis will provide examples of the way in which a Greco-Roman author practiced imitation and rewrote his/her sources. These examples will do two things: (1) they will help establish criteria for detecting literary dependence in Mark, and (2) they will lend credibility to any similar types of rewriting that might be found in Mark's gospel. After devoting chapters two and three to analyzing previous scholarly work on both Mark and imitation and Mark and the Elijah-Elisha narrative, the remaining chapters (four through nine) will compare various sections of Mark's gospel to the Elijah-Elisha narrative in order to determine whether a case for literary dependence and imitation can be made.

---

18. Brodie, *Crucial Bridge*, 86–95; *Birthing*, 147–88. This study proceeds under the conclusion that the Elijah-Elisha narrative begins at 1 Kings 16:29 and ends at 2 Kings 13:29. For a defense of this conclusion, as well as a defense of the unity of this narrative, see Brodie, *Crucial Bridge*, 1–2; one might also note, Conroy, "Hiel between Ahab and Elijah-Elisha," 210–18; Hauser and Gregory, *From Carmel to Horeb*,12; Trible,"Exegesis for Storytellers," 3–4. This study will also primarily consider Mark's use of the LXX rather than the Hebrew Masoretic text.

1

The Imitation of Homer's *Iliad* and *Odyssey* in Virgil's *Aeneid*

INTRODUCTION

THE PURPOSE OF THIS chapter is to analyze the way in which Virgil's *Aeneid* has imitated or rewritten Homer's *Iliad* and *Odyssey*—analysis that will be used both to establish criteria for determining literary dependence between other ancient texts and also to provide literary precedence for the ways in which the Markan evangelist might be using his sources. First, we will begin with an explanation of why we have chosen these works of Homer and Virgil as our starting point. Second, we will analyze six different features/episodes of the *Aeneid*, noting the different ways in which Virgil has adapted his Homeric sources. Third, we will offer a set of criteria for detecting literary dependence in ancient texts.

WHY VIRGIL AND HOMER?

We chose Virgil's use of Homer's *Iliad* and *Odyssey* as our starting point for three distinct reasons. The first reason is that Virgil's literary dependence on Homer's *Iliad* and *Odyssey* in his composition of the *Aeneid* is virtually indisputable and both universally and historically recognized.[1] This fact removes any claim that the similarities between these two texts are simply the result of common and well known oral traditions, or that Virgil was simply influenced by the Homeric themes, characters, and

---

1. Propertius (2.34.65) wrote of Virgil's work, "cedite Romani scriptores, cedite Grai, nescio quid maius nascitur Iliade" ("Make way, Roman authors, make way Greek authors, for a greater Iliad is being written"; translation, my own). See Hardie, "Virgil," 1123–28, esp. 1126; Knauer, "Vergil and Homer," 871–914; idem, *Die Aeneis und Homer*; Farrell, "Virgilian Intertext," 223–38.

episodes that were "in the air" of the Greco-Roman world. Virgil was highly educated and knew the *Iliad* and the *Odyssey* not from hearing them but from reading them. In his *Aeneid*, Virgil is meticulously using these two texts, imitating them and adapting them in his creation of a new Roman epic.

The second reason we have chosen to analyze Virgil's use of Homer is that Virgil is relatively contemporary with the Markan evangelist, writing approximately eighty years before him. This demonstrates that the methods of imitation and adaptation used by Virgil in his composition of the *Aeneid* existed and were known in the ancient world at the time of Mark's composition.

The third reason we have chosen to analyze Virgil's use of Homer is that the *Aeneid* was a well known and popular work in the Roman world, one which was widely read and widely disseminated. It was even used as a school text in the first century (C.E.) to teach Latin grammar and syntax.[2] Though we do not claim that the Markan evangelist was intentionally modeling Virgilian imitation, we do suggest that given the popularity and widespread use of the *Aeneid*—in particular its use as a textbook—he likely would have been aware of the method of Virgilian imitation that is found in it.

VIRGILIAN IMITATION OF THE *ILIAD* AND *ODYSSEY*

Here we consider six different features/episodes of Virgil's *Aeneid* in order to identify and classify ways in which he has imitated or adapted Homer's *Iliad* and *Odyssey*. First, we will begin with a particular feature/episode of the *Iliad/Odyssey* or the *Aeneid* and briefly describe it (with our starting point depending on which episode provides for the easiest comparison). Second, we will discuss the way in which this feature/episode imitates or is imitated by a corresponding Virgilian or Homeric episode. Third, we will clarify and classify the various modes of Virgilian imitation that our analysis has identified.

General Narrative Structure

As we will see, Virgil has imitated the *Iliad* and *Odyssey* in many ways, both at the macro and micro levels. The first feature we will examine of the *Aeneid* and the *Iliad/Odyssey* is on the macro level, namely their gen-

2. Hardie, "Virgil," 1126.

The Imitation of Homer's Iliad *and* Odyssey *in Virgil's* Aeneid

eral narrative structure. The *Iliad* narrates in part the story of the Greeks' war against Troy and their siege of the city Ilium. Though the narrative makes brief references to the beginning of the war and its cause (the Trojan prince Paris' affair with and abduction of the Greek queen Helen) and only foreshadows the war's conclusion (the Greeks' victory), its primary focus is the exploits of Achilles and his role in the military failures and successes of the Greeks. The narrative climax is arguably Achilles victory over Hector in single combat. The *Odyssey* begins after the Greeks' victory over the Trojans and recounts the Greek hero Odysseus' long and hardship-plagued journey home. Once he is home, Odysseus finds his home overrun by suitors who desire his death. With the help of the gods and his son, Odysseus kills his suitors and secures his home

Like the *Odyssey*, the *Aeneid* also begins after the Greeks' victory over the Trojans. But instead of following the sea journey of a victorious Greek hero, it follows the sea journey of a defeated Trojan hero, Aeneas, the son of Venus. Aeneas' home has been overrun by the Greeks, and he must seek a new one. Like the sea journey of Odysseus, the sea journey of Aeneas is long and plagued with hardships. But just as Odysseus finally arrives at his home in Ithaca, Aeneas finally arrives in the land of his future home, Italy. When Aeneas and his fleet of Trojans arrive in Italy, they must fight the current inhabitants to take possession of it. The last half of the *Aeneid* recounts Aeneas' war with the Italians, and it culminates with Aeneas' victory over Turnus in single combat.

The similarities between the general structure of the *Aeneid* and that of the *Iliad* and *Odyssey* are obvious. Virgil has clearly modeled the former on the latter, though he has not done so woodenly or slavishly, but rather quite creatively. He has turned the general narrative structure of the *Iliad* and *Odyssey* on its head, reversing it in his own narrative. This reversal can be seen clearly in the chart below:

Iliad and *Odyssey*: General Structure	*Aeneid*: General Structure
A. War between Greeks and Trojans—climax Achilles defeats Hector (*Iliad*)	C. Home is overrun by outsiders—the Greeks
B. Hardship-plagued sea voyage home (*Odyssey*)	B. Hardship-plagued sea voyage to new home
C. Home overrun by outsiders—the suitors (*Odyssey*)	A. War between Trojans and Italians—climax Aeneas defeats Turnus
D. Old home is restored (*Odyssey*)	D. New home is established

Therefore, we see Virgil depending on the general narrative structure of his primary literary model for the narrative structure of his own work. Yet, we see what might be classified as a reversal of that structure. The same structure is clearly found in both narratives, but its order has been reversed in one author's imitation of another.

Aeneas' Landing at Libya Imitating Odysseus' Landing at Thrinacia and Circe's Island

The *Aeneid* begins with the god Juno instigating the wind god Aeolus to strike Aeneas and his ships with a destructive storm (Book 1). Neptune comes to rescue Aeneas and his fleet, but not until Aeneas has lost all but seven of his ships. After the storm, Aeneas and his remaining ships quickly come to the shores of Libya and find a safe cove in which to harbor. Aeneas climbs a crag to explore the land, and after doing so finds and kills seven large stags. He brings the stags back to his mourning crew, and then along with the food, he gives them words of encouragement, recounting all that they have already been through and reminding them of the home they will eventually find in Italy. As a result of landing in Libya, Aeneas comes to the city of Carthage where he is reunited with all but one of his ships.

Virgil's account of Aeneas landing at Libya is an imitation of two different episodes from the *Odyssey*—Odysseus' landing at Thrinacia (Book 12.260–450) and Odysseus' landing on Circe's Island (Book 10.133–173). Virgil begins his episode by modeling it after Odysseus' landing at Thrinacia. Odysseus' landing at Thrinacia—like Aeneas' landing at Libya—is preceded by a terrible loss at sea, where six of Odysseus' men are eaten by the sea monster Scylla. The description of the place where Aeneas harbors his ships is modeled after the location where Odysseus' ships harbor near Thrinacia. Both episodes describe the waters as "sweet." Both place the ship(s) in a hollow cave. And both describe the presence of nymphs. Virgil then borrows a detail that is common to both Odysseus' landing on Thrinacia and Circe's Island—that of Odysseus leaving his crew to explore their surroundings. But Virgil's account of Aeneas exploring Libya is more closely modeled after Odysseus' exploration of Circe's Island than Odysseus' exploration of Thrinacia. While Aeneas explores Libya, he climbs to a rocky point, just as Odysseus does when he explores Circe's Island. During his exploration, Aeneas kills seven large stags with a bow—a detail that imitates and intensifies the Homeric account

The Imitation of Homer's Iliad *and* Odyssey *in Virgil's* Aeneid

of Odysseus who, while exploring Circe's Island, kills a large stag with a spear. Then Aeneas—like Odysseus—brings the stag meat back to his mourning men.

It is at this point that Virgil stops following the episode of Odysseus' landing on Circe's Island and returns, in a way, to following Odysseus' landing on Thrinacia. When Odysseus returns from his exploration of Thrinacia, he finds that his men have killed and eaten the cattle of Helios the sun god—cattle that his men swore they would not eat. Their destruction is now certain, and when they leave Thrinacia, Zeus destroys their ship with a thunderbolt, leaving Odysseus as the only survivor. Virgil's rewriting of this section is quite radical, but not indiscernible. In fact, here we see a perfect example of Virgil's literary genius. While Virgil dispenses with the details regarding Helios' cattle and the grave mistakes of Odysseus' crew—details that have no place in Virgil's narrative—he does imitated the basic narrative structure that this Odyssean episode provides. However, the features of this narrative structure which are all negative in the Odyssean episode are all positive in the Virgilian episode. First, while Odysseus returns to find his men eating forbidden meat, Aeneas returns to his mourning crew with acceptable meat (the seven stags he has recently killed). Second, while Odysseus discusses the impending doom the gods will bring upon him and his men for eating the forbidden meat, Aeneas encourages the men by reminding them of all they have survived and the gods' promise of a future home. Third, while Odysseus' ship is destroyed by a thunderbolt from Zeus and his crew is lost, Aeneas is led by Venus to Carthage where his lost crew is found.

Virgil's rewriting of these two episodes from the *Odyssey* is laid out clearly in the chart below.

Mark and the Elijah-Elisha Narrative

Odysseus Arrives at Thrinacia (12.260–450)	Odysseus Arrives at Circe's Island (10.133–173)	Aeneas Arrives at Libya (1.157–560)
Suffers Loss: Odysseus has lost six men to the monster Skylla		Suffers Loss: Aeneas has lost all but seven ships in a storm
Description of a Harbor: sweet water, presence of a hollow cave, presence of nymphs		Description of a Harbor: sweet water, presence of a hollow cave, presence of nymphs
Odysseus departs to explore	Odysseus departs to explore	Aeneas departs to explore
	Odysseus climbs a mountain for a better view	Aeneas climbs a mountain for a better view
	Odysseus kills a large stag with his spear	Aeneas kills seven large stags with a bow
Odysseus finds his crew eating forbidden meat	Odysseus brings meat back to his mourning crew	Aeneas brings meat back to his mourning crew
Odysseus foreshadows the crew's future destruction at the hands of the gods		Aeneas foreshadows the crew's future success promised by the gods
Odysseus ship is struck by lighting from Zeus and his ship and its crew are lost		Aeneas is led by Venus to Carthage where his lost ships/crews are restored to him

We see again, that Virgil's imitation of Homer is not wooden or inflexible, but rather it is free and creative. Here we will note the various methods that Virgil uses to imitate his Homeric source. First, and perhaps most notably, Virgil conflates two different stories into one, bringing together details from both Odysseus' landing at Thrinacia and at Circe's Island. He does not keep all the details from both stories, but rather he carefully chooses the details that best fit together to form his new narrative. Second, while Virgil borrows many details from the two Odyssean episodes (e.g., harboring in "sweet water," the presence of nymphs, the hunting of stags, etc.), he uses them in different ways. Homer's description of the location where Odysseus' ship harbors is spread out, with the mention of sweet (fresh) water found in line 12.306 and the cave and nymphs mentioned in

The Imitation of Homer's Iliad *and* Odyssey *in Virgil's* Aeneid

12.317–18 These features are grouped together by Virgil and listed consecutively in lines 1.166–69. Virgil also intensifies the detail of Odysseus killing a stag, as Aeneas kills seven stags—an intensification perhaps necessitated by the number of Aeneas' remaining ships, i.e., seven. Third, while Virgil maintains the basic narrative structure of the Odyssean episodes (i.e., loss of life at sea, arriving in a new land, the hero leaves his crew to explore, the hero returns to encounter crew, the hero foreshadows the crew's future, the future of the crew is actualized), he creatively alters details of the narrative in order to reverse the episode's theme/purpose in his own narrative. Aeneas returns to a mournful crew, not a rebellious one; he foreshadows a promising future, rather than a deadly one; and he is aided by the gods in recovering his ships and crew rather than punished by the gods through the destruction of his ship and crew. Therefore, in summary, we see Virgil's imitation involves conflating two stories into one, selective use/rearrangment of details, intensification of details, and theme reversal.

Aeneas in the Land of the Libyans Imitating Odysseus in the Land of the Phaeacians

In our previous analysis, we looked at Virgil's imitation on a rather small scale, considering how one relatively short Virgilian episode (300–400 lines) incorporated two relatively short Odyssean episodes (200–300 lines). Here we will examine the way in which Virgil's account of Aeneas in Libya—an episode spanning four books (1–4)—imitates Homer's account of Odysseus with the Phaeacians—an episode spanning seven books (6–12).

As noted previously, Virgil's account with Aeneas in Libya begins with a storm begun by Aeolus at the instigation of Juno. After the storm is stilled by Neptune and Aeneas has lost all but seven of his ships, he lands on the coast of Libya. In his initial exploration, he kills seven stags and provides them to his crew. But after these events, Aeneas and Achates are then led by Venus to Carthage. When they enter Carthage they are not recognized, because Venus covers them in a fog. While in Carthage, they see the construction of a large shrine to Juno. The temple's art work contains various depictions of the Trojan War, scenes that bring Aeneas to tears. While Aeneas and Achates are observing the temple, they see members of their own lost crew approach Dido, Queen of Carthage, who is seated on her throne in the temple. They tell the queen how they came to her land, promise their peaceful intentions, and request aid and kindness. The queen recognizes their fame as soldiers of Troy and grants their request for kindness and aid, promising then an escort to wherever they might desire to go. At this point, Aeneas reveals himself and steps from the fog that surrounds him. Dido receives him warmly and welcomes his people to live in Carthage. At a dinner feast, Dido asks Aeneas to recount his sea voyage from Troy, which he does. Soon, at the instigation of the goddess Juno, Dido and Aeneas fall in love. However, Aeneas heeds the warning of the god Mercury and leaves Carthage in order to fulfill the Trojans' destiny in Italy. His departure breaks Dido's heart, and she ultimately kills herself.

This part of Virgil's epic is clearly modeled after Homer's account of Odysseus in the land of the Phaeacians. Here we will examine more closely the way in which Virgil has used this Homeric block. Both stories begin with a storm that brings the respective hero to their destination. The storm in the Odyssey is caused by Poseidon, and Odysseus only survives the storm with the help of Athene and Leucothea—Athene calms the winds and Leucothea provides him with a protective veil. In Virgil's rewriting of this material, gods are also responsible for the storm, but their roles have been somewhat reversed. It is the goddess Juno and the god Aeolus who created the storm, while Neptune (Poseidon) is the one who calms it. Virgil has certainly abbreviated this episode, leaving out any parallel to Odysseus' encounter with Leucothea, his decision about abandoning his raft, or his danger of being smashed on the rocks. Yet, that Virgil is imitating the storm and its divine instigation in this Homeric episode seems clear.

The events immediately following the two heroes' arrivals at their respective destinations differ significantly. As we have already noted, Aeneas climbs to a rocky point to explore, kills seven stags, and returns to feed and encourage his crew. We have already demonstrated this material is dependent on two different Odyssean episodes, and is independent of Odysseus' time among the Phaeacians. After Odysseus comes to shore in the land of the Phaeacians, he, at the orchestration of Athene, meets the daughter of the Phaeacian king, Nausicaa. They both agree that it would be better, for the sake of modesty, if Odysseus came to the house of the king on his own and not with the king's daughter. Therefore, Odysseus does not set out for the king's house until after the king's daughter has de-

The Imitation of Homer's Iliad *and* Odyssey *in Virgil's* Aeneid

parted for home. This account of Odysseus and Nausicaa has no parallel in Virgil's narrative, and apparently has been completely omitted by him.

Virgil's account of Aeneas and Achates going to Carthage is clearly modeled on Odysseus going to the home of the Phaeacian king. Aeneas and Achates are led to Carthage by the disguised goddess Venus, while Odysseus is led to the Phaeacian king's home by the disguised goddess Athene. In both epics, the goddesses also cover the respective heroes with a fog so that they will not be recognized. Virgil has actually expanded this element of Homer's narrative, including a long dialogue between Aeneas and Venus, with the dialogue ending with Aeneas' recognition of his mother—Odysseus never recognizes Athene in the Homeric episode.

After Aeneas and Achates enter Carthage, they see a shrine that is being built for the goddess Juno. But particular attention is given to the artwork of the temple which visually recounts the events of the Trojan War. This Virgilian account imitates two accounts that occur during Odysseus' time among the Phaeacians. While Odysseus is feasting with the Phaeacians—his identity yet unknown—the muse Demodocus twice sings of the events of the Trojan War. These respective reminders of the Trojan War lead both Odysseus and Aeneas to tears. Here Virgil is quite creative in his imitation. While he maintains the arts as the vehicle to convey events of the Trojan War, he changes the particular artistic mode, i.e., from song to visual art. Naturally, because the central figure of the narrative is a Trojan and not a Greek, Virgil changes the perspective of the war's retelling. While the Homeric retelling presents the Greeks in a positive light and highlights their significant accomplishments, the Virgilian retelling highlights the heroism of the Trojans and the barbarism of the Greeks. It is also noteworthy that Virgil changes the position of this account in his imitation of Odysseus' time among the Phaeacians. While Homer puts this account after Odysseus has already been welcome by the Phaeacian king and is feasting with him, Virgil moves the story forward, placing it before Aeneas ever meets the queen Dido. Therefore, while Virgil finds it important to maintain this account, he feels the freedom to move it around in the narrative's overall sequence—providing yet another example of the freedom Virgil takes in his method of imitation.

After observing the artwork of Juno's shrine, Aeneas and Achates see their lost crew approaching the queen Dido and asking here for safety and aid. Dido notes the fame of the Trojan warriors (as well as that of Aeneas) and grants their request, promising an escort to where ever they might go.

With this story, Virgil is imitating Odysseus' supplication to the Phaeacian king Alcinous and his wife Arete, both of whom after hearing Odysseus' story grant his request for hospitality and an escort back to Ithaca. It is interesting here that in his imitation Virgil creates a role reversal. Virgil usually imitates Odysseus with the character of Aeneas. But in this particular instance, he has imitated Odysseus with Aeneas' crew rather than Aeneas himself. Again we see that Virgil does not confine himself to a set of hard and fast rules, but is willing to break with his general imitative pattern if doing so better advances his narrative.

Again, Virgil departs from the Homeric narrative, leaving out of his imitation numerous narrative elements. After Odysseus makes supplication to the king and queen, he is taken in and spends two nights with them. He feasts with the Phaeacians and participates in games with them (though only reluctantly). It is not until the second day, that he reveals his identity at the request of the king and his court. Virgil has left all of these details out of his narrative, and immediately follows Dido's interaction with Aeneas' crew with Aeneas' self-revelation—a revelation that parallels Odysseus' own self-revelation to the Phaeacian King.

The self-revelations of both Aeneas and Odysseus are followed by the two characters recounting their respective sea voyages. Here, Virgil is certainly continuing to model the general narrative structure of Odysseus' time among the Phaeacians, but his recounting of Aeneas' sea voyage is quite different in detail and structure than that of Odysseus' parallel voyage. Aeneas and Odysseus share very few of the same experiences on their respective voyages. Odysseus faces one hardship after another, with his voyage ultimately ending in the death of his entire crew and the loss of all his ships. While Aeneas' voyage does include some hardship, the hardships are less severe than those of Odysseus. Aeneas' voyage is also characterized by foreshadowings of his future success and attempts to rehabilitate the Trojans (e.g., the Trojan Helenus' [son of Priam] succession of the Greek King Pyrrhus' [the one who killed Priam]). In a number of ways, Virgil uses the retelling of the sea voyage to demonstrate Aeneas' superiority to Odysseus. While Odysseus is presented as a destroyer of cities—he and his men, without provocation, destroy Ismaros in Thrace—Aeneas is presented as a founder of cities—he and his crew plant a city in the region of Thrace. While Odysseus must decide between two evils, Scylla and Charybdis, Aeneas finds a path around them. And while Odysseus and his men are captured (and some eaten) by the Cyclops Polyphemus,

The Imitation of Homer's Iliad *and* Odyssey *in Virgil's* Aeneid

Aeneas and his men avoid capture and, in fact, rescue one of Odysseus' men whom Odysseus had left behind. Ultimately, while Odysseus' voyage ends with the loss of his men and ships, Aeneas' voyage ends with the finding of all his ships. Also of note, the Odyssean sea voyage contains an episode in which Odysseus journeys to Hades and converses with the dead. Virgil has moved this episode out of his recounting of Aeneas' sea voyage, and placed his imitation of the episode later in his narrative (Book VI).

After the telling of Aeneas' sea voyage, Virgil temporarily breaks from imitating Odysseus' stay among the Phaeacians and partially imitates Odysseus' relationship with Calypso. Like Odysseus and Calypso, Aeneas and Dido have sexual relations. And like Calypso with Odysseus, Dido falls in love with Aeneas. Calypso desires that Odysseus would take her as his wife, while Dido believes that Aeneas has taken her for his wife. Neither Odysseus nor Aeneas equally reciprocated the love of these women and both finally decide to depart from them. Both women plead for the men to stay but to no avail.

Virgil then returns to imitating the account of Odysseus with the Phaeacians, though the imitation becomes less distinct. Odysseus departs with the Phaeacians, while Aeneas leaves with his many ships. The departure of both men brings about tragedy to the people they leave. After the Phaeacians bring Odysseus to Ithaca, Poseidon turns their ship into a large rock just before it reached Phaeacia. After Aeneas departs from Carthage with his people, Dido commits suicide, leaving her people in mourning.

The outline of Virgil's imitation of Odysseus among the Phaeacians can be seen in the chart below.

Odysseus among the Phaeacians (Books 6–12)	Aeneas among the Libyans (Books 1–4)
a. Odysseus is brought to Phaeacia by a storm. b. The storm is caused by Poseidon (Neptune). c. Odysseus is rescued by Athene.	a. Aeneas is brought to Libya by a storm. b. The storm is caused by Aeolus (at the instigation of Juno). c. Aeneas is rescued by Neptune (Poseidon).
See Landing on Thrinacia and Circe's Island in the previous analysis	Initial exploration, killing of seven stags, encouraging men, etc. (see previous chart)

Odysseus among the Phaeacians (Books 6–12)	Aeneas among the Libyans (Books 1–4)
Odysseus' encounter with Nausicaa	
Odysseus enters the Phaeacian city in secrecy and is led by Athene to the kings home—Athene surrounds him in a fog.	Aeneas and Achates are led to Carthage by Venus and in secrecy enter—Venus surrounds them with a fog.
	Aeneas sees the events of the Trojan War displayed in the art work of a Carthagean temple—he weeps in response.
Odysseus requests aid from the Phaeacian King (Alcinous).	Aeneas' lost crew (who have also found Carthage) requests aid from Queen Dido.
Odysseus is cared for and offered aid by the Phaeacians and tells of his journey from Calypso's island.	After hearing the story of Aeneas' crew, Dido offers them aid.
Alcinous suggests Odysseus' marriage to Nausicaa.	
Odysseus is challenged to participate in games—throwing the discuss.	
Odysseus hears the events of the Trojan War sung by a muse—he weeps.	See Aeneas' weeping over the Trojan War above.
Odysseus is asked to reveal his identity, which he does.	Aeneas reveals himself to Dido and his crew.
	Juno schemes to cause Dido and Aeneas to fall in love.
Odysseus tells of his long sea voyage.	Aeneas tells of his long sea voyage.
Odysseus and Kalypso: a. Kalypso loves Odysseus b. Kalypso desires to marry Odysseus c. Kalypso pleads Odysseus not to leave	Aeneas and Dido: a. Dido loves Aeneas b. Dido perceives her relationship to Aeneas as marriage c. Dido pleads Aeneas not to leave.
Odysseus leaves the Phaeacians—Poseidon turns into a stone the ship that bore him away.	Aeneas leaves Carthage—Dido, who is in love with Aeneas, commits suicide.

Again, we see that Virgil's imitation of Homer is free and creative. Ultimately Virgil follows the literary structure of Odysseus' time among

The Imitation of Homer's Iliad *and* Odyssey *in Virgil's* Aeneid

the Phaeacians. But even though Virgil follows a primary Homeric episode for his imitation, again we see that he conflates other episodes with this primary one, i.e., Odysseus on the Island of Circe and Odysseus' relationship with Calypso. We also see that Virgil is again selective in the details he maintains from the stories he is imitating. He does not feel the need to slavishly imitate every detail, but omits many details and events that do not fit his narrative purposes. Again, we also see the reversal of details in Virgil's imitation. While Homer uses Poseidon *to cause the storm* that brings Odysseus to the island of the Phaeacians, Virgil uses Neptune/Poseidon *to stop the storm* that brings Aeneas to the Libyans. The roles of characters are also reversed. Virgil does not use Aeneas to imitate Odysseus' supplication to the Phaeacian king, but rather he uses the lost members of Aeneas' crew. This point is noteworthy because throughout the entire epic, Virgil is presenting Aeneas as a second Odysseus. It is important to note that Virgil feels free to break from this dominant motif if doing better so suits his narrative. Virgil also creatively alters details in his imitation. For example, he changes the artistic medium of communicating the events of the Trojan War from song to painting. We also see a new element in Virgil's imitation, namely an attempt to show the superiority of his central character Aeneas over the Homeric central character, Odysseus. Therefore, we again see that Virgil's imitation of Homer uses a number of creative tools, including the conflation of stories, the reversal of details, the creative alteration of details, and the enhancement of the central character.

The Games in Honor of Anchises Imitating the Games in Honor of Patroclus

In book five of the *Aeneid*, Aeneas decides to honor the one year anniversary of his father's death by holding a series of games. These games imitate the episode in the Iliad (Book 23.257–895) in which Achilles organizes games in honor of his close friend Patroclus who was killed in battle by Hector. Here we will only offer a broad analysis of Virgil's imitation of this Homeric episode, leaving a more specific analysis of one particular game until the next section. In the Homeric episode, there are eight different competitions that occur in the following order: (1) a chariot race; (2) a boxing match; (3) a wrestling contest; (4) a foot race; (5) an armored battle; (6) an iron toss; (7) an archery contest; and (8) a spear throwing contest. In his imitation, Virgil has reduced the number of total competitions to four: (1) a ship race; (2) a foot race; (3) a boxing match; and (4) an archery contest. Along with reducing the number of competitions, Virgil has both altered their order slightly and also replaced one competition with a new one. For some reason, Virgil places the foot race before the boxing match. He also replaces the chariot race with a ship race—a change that perhaps reflects the different settings of the stories, i.e., the episode of the *Iliad* is set in and around a land war where chariots figure prominently, while the contrasting episode of the *Aeneid* is set in and around a sea voyage where ships figure prominently. Before the beginning of these games, both Achilles and Aeneas set forth prizes which are given out after each competition. In both stories these prizes include caldrons, tripods, gold, armor, and women. But Virgil adds additional prizes (perhaps as a form of intensification) that include talents of silver, green garlands, and purple garments.

From this example, we again see a number of Virgilian methods of imitation. Again a primary Homeric episode is imitated, but Virgil alters the episodes in a number of ways. He omits a number of the games, reducing the total number from eight to four. He also rearranges the order of the games, transposing the footrace and the boxing match. He also changes the medium of one race, i.e. a chariot race to a ship race, to better fit his narrative setting. He also broadens the scope of the prizes, possibly for the purpose of intensification.

The Boxing Match between Dares and Entellus Imitating the Boxing Match between Epeios and Euryalos

We will now look more closely at one of the competitions noted above and consider how Virgil has imitated the boxing match recorded in the *Iliad*. The Homeric account begins with the presentation of prizes—an unbroken female donkey for the winner and a two handled goblet for the loser. The first volunteer to fight is Epeios, who is described as tall and stout, as well as a skilled boxer. He places his hands on the donkey and makes a bold speech in which he describes his impending victory as well as his victim's painful fate. The onlookers are silent, and initially no one is willing to take the challenge. Finally, Euryalos, one who is described as godlike and a skilled boxer, steps forward. After a quick flurry of punches from both men, Epeios lands a crushing blow to the cheek that knocks

The Imitation of Homer's Iliad *and* Odyssey *in Virgil's* Aeneid

Euryalos to the ground leaving him unconscious. Epeios helps Euryalos up and the friends of the fallen fighter carry him—while he is still semi-unconscious and spitting up blood—to his tent. His friends later bring him the double handled goblet, his consolation prize.

In the Virgilian account, Aeneas, like Odysseus, brings out the prizes—a bull dressed in gold and garlands for the winner and a sword and stately helmet for the loser. Quickly, Dares comes forward to fight. Like Epeios, he is described as a large and powerful man as well as one skilled in boxing. As in the Homeric account, no contender comes forward. As a result, Dares, like Epeios, takes hold of the prize and claims that since there are no challengers the prize should be his. But finally the aged hero Entellus, after being goaded by Acestes, steps forward to fight. Though aged, he is described as large and powerful as well as a once powerful boxer in his prime. As in the Homeric episode both fighters exchange blows. Dares is described as moving quickly on his feet, while Entellus is described as slack-kneed, tottering, and gasping. A large punch by Entellus misses Dares and exerts such force that Entellus falls to the ground. But after being helped to his feet, Entellus attacks Dares with fury, landing heavy blow after heavy blow. Aeneas finally must end the fight to spare Dares further harm. Dares is led by his friends to the ships—while he, like Euryalos of the Odyssey, is semi-conscious and spitting up blood. Dares' friends later bring him the helmet and sword, his consolation prize. Entellus takes his prize, kills it, and offers it in remembrance to Eryx, the deceased stepbrother of Aeneas.

Here, we again find another creative example of Virgilian imitation. Virgil has kept the basic Homeric literary structure but has then added his own dramatic twist. Both stories begin with a boastful but powerful contestant who tries to claim his prize too early. In both stories, the onlookers are initially silent and challengers are reluctant. In both stories, a challenger who appears inferior steps forward to fight. But it is at this point that the stories diverge. In the Homeric episode, the inferior challenger is quickly defeated, and the initial boasts of the superior fighter prove to be well founded. But Virgil reverses this ending. It is the fighter initially presumed to be inferior that wins the match, and dramatically so after he initially falls down. This reversal is made complete, when the boastful fighter of the Virgilian episode shares the same fate as the inferior fighter of Homeric episode—both are brought to their dwelling place semi-unconscious and spitting up blood. This reversal changes the entire theme of the Homeric episode. Instead of promoting the proud, youthful, and arrogant warrior, Virgil promotes the humble, experienced, and elderly warrior. The following chart depicts this imitation clearly.

Boxing Match: Epeios vs. Euryalos (23.664–699)	Boxing Match: Dares vs. Entellus (5.362–484)
Presentation of Prizes (male bull and sword with armor	Presentation of Prizes (female donkey and double handled goblet
Powerful/skilled boxer steps forward	Powerful/skilled boxer steps forward
First volunteer boasts of victory—seeks to claim his prize	First volunteer boasts of victory—seeks to claim his prize
Initial silence from onlookers	Initial silence from onlookers
A reluctant and inferior challenger volunteers to fight (the fighter is much smaller)	A reluctant and inferior challenger volunteers to fight (the fighter is old)
The inferior fighter is quickly knocked unconscious	The inferior fighter appears overmatched and falls down
	The inferior fighter retaliates in anger and knocks the superior fighter unconscious
The defeated fighter is carried back to his dwelling by his friends—he is semi-unconscious and spitting up blood.	The defeated fighter is carried back to his dwelling by his friends—he is semi-unconscious and spitting up blood.
The second place prize is brought to the dwelling of the defeated fighter.	The second place prize is brought to the dwelling of the defeated fighter.

Virgil's Imitation of Elpenor's Death and Burial

To this point, Virgil's imitation of Homer has been relatively straightforward. He has begun with a primary Homeric episode and creatively reshaped it.[3] The resulting narrative is—at least in broad strokes—like the primary Homeric episode it imitates, i.e., a single unit. But Virgil's imitation of the Homeric account of Elpenor's death and burrial departs from this pattern. While he begins with a single primary Homeric episode—Elpenor's death and burial—he does not reproduce a correspond-

---

3. One exception we have seen to this Virgilian imitative pattern is Virgil's bringing together two different landings of Odysseus to form a single landing of Aeneas—see pages 14–17 above.

The Imitation of Homer's Iliad *and* Odyssey *in Virgil's* Aeneid

ing single primary episode.[4] Instead, Virgil has taken the raw material of this Homeric account and used it in the construction of a handful of different episodes. Here we begin by recounting the Homeric episode of Elpenor and then consider how Virgil has imitated this episode in his own narrative.

Elpenor was the youngest member of Odysseus' crew. One evening after becoming drunk, he fell asleep on the roof of Circe's house. When morning came, he was awakened by the clamoring and shouting of Odysseus' men who were preparing to depart from Circe's island. In his dazed state, he went to join the men, but not realizing he was on the roof, he fell off, broke his neck, and was left undiscovered and unburied. Odysseus and his crew depart and descend to Hades. While in Hades the first person that Odysseus encounters is Elpenor (Books 10–11) who explains how he died and requests that Odysseus return to Circe's island to bury him—a request that Odysseus grants. After Odysseus' journey through Hades, he returns to Circe's island and buries Elpenor.

The first Virgilian imitation of this Homeric episode is found at the end of book five with the death of Palinurus. Palinurus, a member of Aeneas' crew, is steering a ship while the rest of the crew sleeps. As he is steering, he becomes tired, falls asleep, falls into the sea, and drowns. Palinurus' death is an imitation of Elpenor's death. Both are crew members of the central character. Both of their deaths are related to sleep. And both deaths involve falling. That Virgil intends the death of Palinurus to imitate that of Elpenor, is confirmed when Palinurus later meets Aeneas in Hades—a meeting that parallels Elpenor's meeting with Odysseus.

The second Virgilian imitation of the Elpenor episode comes in book six, shortly after Aeneas and his crew have landed in Italy. A Sibyl tells Aeneas that one of his friends is dead but remains unburied. He soon finds his comrade Misenus (son of King Aeolus) lying dead on the beach. Aeneas' burial of Misenus clearly imitates Odysseus' burial of Elpenor. The following details that are shared by both episodes should be noted: (1) there is great mourning for both men; (2) logs are cut to build pyre for both men; (3) both men are burned—Elpenor in his armor and Misenus in royal purple; (4) a great tomb is erected for both men; (5) an oar is

---

4. While Elpenor's death, request for burial, and burial are technically separated by other narrative elements (e.g., the description of Odysseus journey to Hades and Odysseus' conversation with other dead beings), the three events follow relatively close to each other essentially forming a narrative unit.

used to mark both tombs; and (6) both funeral scenes take place on a seashore.

Virgil continues his imitation of the Homeric account of Elpenor when Aeneas meets the deceased Palinurus in Hades. This encounter is clearly imitating Elpenor's conversation with Odysseus in Hades, which we noted previously. As with Elpenor and Odysseus, Palinurus is the first person Aeneas meets. He is also (like Elpenor) among the dead who have not yet been buried. Like Elpenor, Palinurus explains how he died and requests that Aeneas either finds and buries his body or takes him across the river Styx into Hades. Palinurus is then promised by a priestess that those who have his body will be punished until it receives a proper burial.

Finally, Virgil concludes his imitation of the Elpenor episode by recording a burial after Aeneas' return from Hades. But it is not the burial of Palinurus, a burial that is never described in the Aeneid. Instead, Virgil records the burial of Aeneas' nurse Caieta.

The imitation described above is laid out clearly in the following chart.

Homer's Odyssey	**Virgil's Aeneid**		
Elpenor Episode (Book 10–11)	Palinurus Episode (5.827–71; 6.337–83)	Misenus Episode (6.156–235)	Caieta Episode (7.1–7)
Elpenor awakes from his sleep and falls from the roof of a house to his death.	Palinurus falls asleep and falls from a boat to his death in the sea.		
Elpenor meets Odysseus in Hades—he explains how he dies and begs for a burial.	Palinurus meets Aeneas in Hades—he explains how he died and begs for a burial.		

The Imitation of Homer's Iliad *and* Odyssey *in Virgil's* Aeneid

Homer's Odyssey	Virgil's Aeneid		
Elpenor Episode (Book 10–11)	Palinurus Episode (5.827–71; 6.337–83)	Misenus Episode (6.156–235)	Caieta Episode (7.1–7)
Odysseus returns to Circe's island and fulfills his promise to Elpenor—he mourns, cuts logs for a pyre, burns the body, and erects a grave marked with an oar.	Palinurus' burial is never described in the Aeneid.	Aeneas finds Misenus' body—he mourns, cuts logs for a pyre, burns the body, erects a grave marked with an oar. (this event occurs before Aeneas goes to Hades)	After leaving Hades, Aeneas buries his nurse, Caieta.

In Virgil's imitation of the Homeric episode of Elpenor, we see Virgil using imitative techniques we have not yet seen before. He essentially turns one Homeric character into three, i.e., Elpenor becomes Palinurus, Misenus, and Caieta. He also takes the events of one Homeric episode and diffuses them into three different episodes. In addition to these new techniques, we again see Virgil altering narrative details to better fit his own narrative setting and purpose.

Summarizing Virgil's Imitative Techniques

After examining a number of examples of Virgil's imitation of Homer, we can now summarize the different imitative techniques that we have seen Virgil use. Conflation of stories is an imitative technique that we find in Virgil. He often combines details or structural elements from two or more stories into a single narrative unit. For example, Virgil combines details from the episode of Odysseus landing on Circe's Island and the episode of Odysseus landing in Thrinacia into the episode of Aeneas landing in Libya. Virgil also uses the technique of reversal in his imitation. This technique finds many expressions, including the reversal of narrative structure (e.g., the entire *Aeneid* reverses the structure of the *Iliad* and *Odyssey*), theme (e.g., see Virgil's imitation of the boxing match between Epeios and Euryalos), ordered events (e.g., see Virgil's imitation of the games in honor of Patroclus), and even character's roles (e.g., see Virgil's imitation of Odysseus' supplication to the King of Phaeacia). Virgil also uses the technique of diffusion, by which he takes a single episode or character and divides it into multiple episodes or characters (e.g., see Virgil's imitation of the Palinurus' death and burial). Omission is another common imitative technique of Virgil. His imitation of a particular episode never demands that he imitate all details. He also regularly alters details of a particular episode to better fit his narrative context (e.g., he alters the artistic medium of conveying the events of the Trojan War from song to visual art). Finally, we also see Virgil using the technique of intensification, by which he might increase the number or grandeur of a particular detail in the imitated text, (e.g., Aeneas kills seven large stags while he is exploring Libya, while Odysseus kills only one large stag while exploring Circe's Island).

VIRGIL'S USE OF HOMER AS A WAY OF ESTABLISHING CRITERIA FOR DETERMINING LITERARY DEPENDENCE

After examining Virgil's use of Homer, we should be able to establish some basic criteria for determining literary dependence between two texts. These criteria could then help establish literary relationships between other ancient texts.

Plausibility of Imitation

This criterion asks whether it is plausible that one author could be dependent on another. It considers the date of composition of both the imitating and imitated text, i.e., was the proposed imitated text actually in existence before the imitating text. It also considers the availability of the imitated text for the imitating author, i.e., is it feasible that the imitating author had access to the imitated text. Clearly the criterion of plausibility must be met in order for further investigation to proceed.

Similarities in Narrative Structures/Order of Events

In our examination of Virgil's use of Homer, we repeatedly see similarities in narrative structure. Virgil often chooses a primary narrative to imitate, and he builds his imitation around the structure of that narrative. For example, both Virgil's account of Aeneas among the Libyans and Homer's account of Odysseus among the Phaeacians follow the same general narrative structure: (1) arrival aided by a storm; (2) entrance to city in

The Imitation of Homer's Iliad and Odyssey in Virgil's Aeneid

secrecy; (3) request for aid; (4) interaction with local ruler; (5) recounting of a sea voyage; (6) departure after a brief stay; and (7) tragedy for the hosting people. Certainly Virgil's account differs from Homer's in many ways (see our analysis above), but it is clear that he is using Homer's narrative structure in the creation of his own narrative.

For two reasons, a shared narrative structure between two texts should be considered a strong indicator of literary dependence. One, the imitation of narrative structure was a known and used imitative technique, as is evidenced by Virgil. Two, the chances of two stories arriving independently at two similar narrative structures is extremely low. The more complicated the shared narrative structure is the lower the chances are that the two structures are independent of each other. Therefore, if two stories share a similar narrative structure, it is highly probably that literary dependence exists between them. The more complex that shared structure is the more likely dependence is.

We must remember that the imitating author has the freedom to alter the narrative structure if he/she sees fit. Therefore, we might see similar narrative structures, but not necessarily the same narrative structures. At times an author might omit an element of the imitated narrative structure (or add one to it) or he/she might reverse the particular order of the narrative structure. Such alterations do not undermine dependence, but simply demonstrate the freedom that existed in the process of imitation. As long as discernible similarities exist between the two narrative structures, literary dependence is probable.

Similarities in Specific Narrative Details and Actions

In Virgil's imitation of Homer, we often see similarities in specific details and actions. We offer two examples of such shared details and actions. Both Virgil's episode of Misenus' burial and Homer's episode of Elpenor's burial follow a similar narrative structure: (1) mourning for the deceased; (2) the cutting of logs for the pyre; (3) the burning of the bodies; and (4) the erecting of a tomb. Similarities in narrative structure strongly suggest literary dependence. But Virgil's inclusion of specific details makes this literary dependence certain. He maintains the setting of the Homeric episode, namely along the shore of the sea. Yet, even more telling, is the placement of an oar to mark the graves of both Elpenor and Misenus. This detail has no other explanation than a Virgilian attempt to imitate

Homer. A second example can be seen in Aeneas' arrival in Libya. Aeneas hunts and kills seven white stags as he is exploring the Libyan shores. This action make's it quite clear that Virgil is dependent on Homer's *Odyssey*, in which Odysseus, while initially exploring Circe's island, kills a large white stag.

Because the likelihood is low that the two authors would include the same specific details or actions independently of each other, we conclude that similarities between the specific narrative details/actions of two texts are an indicator of literary dependence. The more specific details or actions that are shared between two texts, the greater the probability that dependence exists. This probability increases if the details are unexplainable apart from literary dependence.

Verbal Agreement

Because Virgil and Homer are writing in two different languages there is no verbal agreement between them. But clearly this lack of verbal agreement does not undermine literary dependence. This point is particularly important for the field of New Testament studies, a field that for far too long has operated under the false assumption that verbal agreement and verbal agreement alone is necessary to establish literary dependence. The reality is that most imitating authors wanted to avoid verbal agreement, and direct copying of an imitated work was not as admirable as creative imitation.[5] As the gospels demonstrate, literary dependence is at times evidenced through verbal agreement, but such agreement is not essential for literary dependence to be established. The existence of verbal agreement or the presence of the common words can certainly be used as evidence for literary dependence—strong evidence indeed. However, it should never be considered the only acceptable evidence—at times it may not be the primary evidence.

The Weight of Combined Criteria

It is certainly possible that one particular criterion could be strong enough to demonstrate literary dependence, i.e., complex or numerous similarities in narrative structure or a large number of specific details common to both stories. Yet, the case is always more certain when there is a combination of criteria. If two narratives share a number of specific details and

---

5. See Fiske, *Lucilius and Horace*, 27.

also share similar narrative structures, literary dependence is highly probable and perhaps undeniable. The weight of combined criteria, therefore, is the most convincing evidence of literary dependence, and it cannot be ignored.

Do Differences Matter?

After examining Virgil's imitation of Homer, we see that there are regularly differences between the imitating text and the imitated text (e.g., differences in narrative structure, details, themes, etc.). Sometimes these differences are easily explained. Perhaps they are demanded by the world of the new narrative, needed to advance a unique thematic concern of the author, or used to promote the greatness of an imitating character over an imitated character. But these differences are not always easily explained, and at times an author's reason for changing the imitated text is completely indiscernible. Regardless of whether or not the differences between two text are explainable, such differences in and of themselves do not undermine a conclusion for literary dependence. A decision for literary dependence needs to be made on the basis of the similarities between two texts, similarities we have outlined above. However, differences can (and perhaps should) be considered as evidence against literary dependence if they outweigh the similarities between two texts in both quantity and significance. A handful of minor similarities between two largely differing texts is clearly not enough to prove literary dependence.

2

Mark and Imitation

INTRODUCTION

BY AND LARGE, THE ancient practice of literary imitation (*mimesis, imitatio*) has been ignored in efforts to identify the source material of biblical books. Efforts to identify Markan source material are not exceptional in this regard. However, one recent attempt has been made to use imitation for identifying Markan sources. Dennis MacDonald has produced a monograph in which he argues that Homer's *Iliad* and *Odyssey* are the primary literary models on which Mark's gospel is based; or rather that Mark's gospel, much like Virgil's *Aeneid*, is a creative imitation of Homeric epics.[1] Any attempt to explore imitation by the Markan evangelist must consider MacDonald's significant work on the subject, evaluate its strengths and weaknesses, and consider its ramifications for further exploration. It is to this task that we now turn our attention.

DENNIS MACDONALD'S *THE HOMERIC EPICS AND THE GOSPEL OF MARK*: A SUMMARY

MacDonald begins his argument for Mark's imitation of Homeric epics by establishing two important points: (1) the ubiquity of Homer in the Greco-Roman world, and (2) the popularity of Homer as an imitative model. He rightly notes that Homer was used as a textbook to teach children the alphabet and that students could not move on to other books until they had demonstrated mastery of the *Iliad* and the *Odyssey*.[2]

---

1. MacDonald, *Homeric Epics*.

2. Ibid., 4. Here MacDonald cites two significant works on this subject matter: Bonner, *Education in Ancient Rome*, and Marrou, *Education in Antiquity*. MacDonald also has a more thorough discussion of ancient author's use of Homer in his earlier work *Christianizing Homer*, 17–22.

He also notes that both the poetic style and narrative detail of these two epics was imitated broadly, and was a literary practice that included not only Greco-Roman authors, but Jewish authors as well.[3] Clearly this evidence suggests that an educated author such as the Markan evangelist would be familiar with these Homeric epics and so would have had significant precedence for imitating them.

MacDonald proposes that Mark has cleverly, imaginatively, and subtly imitated Homer, modelling the first thirteen chapters primarily on the *Odyssey* and the last three primarily on the *Iliad*. He proposes six criteria be used to demonstrate this imitation.[4] The first two criteria, accessibility and analogy, are clearly established by MacDonald at the outset of the work. Accessibilty asks did the author of the hypertext (the imitating text) have access to the hypotext (the text being imitated)? Analogy asks, was imitation of the hypotext common in the ancient world? The third criterion is that of density, a criterion that considers the weight or bulk of parallels or similarities between two texts—in particular those parallels of significance rather than those of a trivial nature. The fourth criterion is that of order, a criterion that considers the sequence of parallels found in two texts. The fifth criterion is distinctiveness, a criterion that considers similarities such as "peculiar characterizations" or "an unusual word or phrase."[5] The sixth criterion is interpretability, a criterion that determines whether the differences that exist between the two texts can be adequately explained.

MacDonald begins his analysis of Mark's imitation of Homer not by comparing specific Markan pericopes with specific Homeric episodes, but by establishing between the two works similarities in characterization, theme, and plot structure. His starting point is the share motif of a suffering central character—the Markan Jesus imitates the Homeric Odysseus. According to MacDonald, the suffering Odysseus makes a convenient and well known model for the suffering Jesus of Mark's gospel. It is from this basic similarity between Jesus and Odysseus that MacDonald feels the

---

3. MacDonald notes that Apollonius of Rhodes' *Argonautica*, Virgil's *Aeneid*, Quintus Smyrnaeus' *Posthomerica*, and Nonnos of Panopolis' *Dionysiaca* all contain significant imitation of the *Iliad* and *Odyssey*. Jewish works including Theodotus' *On the Jews*, Philo Epicus' *On Jerusalem*, and even the *Book of Tobit* contain Homeric imitation; see *Homeric Epics*, 4–5.

4. For MacDonald's explanation of these criterion, see *Homeric Epics*, 8–9.

5. MacDonald, *Homeric Epics*, 8.

rest of Mark's imitation of Homer grows. Not only do both suffer, but both are presented as suffering while on a journey home. Both are opposed by supernatural beings—Odysseus by Circe, Polyphemus, and Poseidon, and Jesus by Satan and demons. Both are plagued with foolish and flawed followers—Odysseus by his crew and Jesus by his twelve disciples. Both must face murderous usurpers—Odysseus faces the suitors of Penelope and Jesus faces the religious authorities.

After establishing these general similarities in theme, characterization, and plot structure, MacDonald devotes ten chapters to examining the similarities between specific Markan pericopes and specific Homeric episodes. For example, he demonstrates similarities between Mark's account of the Gerasene demoniac and Odysseus' encounter with the Cyclops Polyphemus. He also notes many similarities between Mark's account of the Last Supper and Odysseus' last meal before journeying to Hades. In light of his analysis, MacDonald concludes that Mark has indeed used Homeric episodes as the primary model for not only many of his pericopes, but also for his gospel as a whole. He acknowledges that differences certainly exist between the two texts, but these differences can—by and large—be explained by Markan transvaluation of Homer. That is to say, through his imitation, Mark is improving on Homeric values and Homeric characters. While Markan imitation is often subtle, he argues that it is clearly present and that Mark intended his readers to perceive it.

DENNIS MACDONALD'S *THE HOMERIC EPICS AND THE GOSPEL OF MARK*: AN EVALUATION

MacDonald's work has certainly not lacked critics, and though its significance has certainly not come to full fruition, his work on the whole has convinced few Markan interpreters.[6] Here we will offer our own evaluation of MacDonald's work, beginning with its strengths and then considering its weaknesses.

---

6. For formal critiques of MacDonald's work, see the following reviews: Hooker, review of Dennis MacDonald, *Homeric Epics and the Gospel of Mark*, 196–98; Hock, review of Dennis MacDonald, *Homeric Epics and the Gospel of Mark*, 363–67; Nolland, review of Dennis MacDonald, *Homeric Epics and the Gospel of Mark*, 134–35; Dowd, review of Dennis MacDonald, *Homeric Epics and the Gospel of Mark*, 155–56; Gilmour, review of Dennis MacDonald, *Homeric Epics and the Gospel of Mark*; Sandnes, "*Imitatio Homeri?*" 715–32.

Strengths

We must acknowledge that in this work MacDonald has made a number of strikingly new and fresh contributions to the field of Markan and New Testament research. First, he has brought the ancient literary practice of *mimesis*/imitation—a practice that was ubiquitous in the ancient writing—to bear on the study of early Christian narratives. As we have previously noted, it is stunning that so few New Testament interpreters pay attention to an ancient writing practice that has direct and significant implications for their field of research. If for nothing else, MacDonald's work should be praised for shining a light on the relevance of this common writing practice to the study of the gospels.

Second, he has demonstrated the ubiquity of the Homeric epics in the ancient world and has persuasively argued that that ubiquity demands that these epics be considered in the study of any ancient Greco-Roman narrative. Again, it is shocking how few New Testament interpreters have considered the influence of Homer upon the New Testament authors—some of whom certainly received an education that was steeped in the study of Homeric epics. Hopefully, MacDonald's work will serve to bring awareness to the importance of these epics for New Testament studies.

Third, MacDonald has provided Markan interpreters with a storehouse of Homeric themes, characters, episodes, and details that provide intriguing parallels and background information to many features of Mark's gospel. Even if one does not agree with the ultimate thesis of MacDonald's work, one is at least provided with numerous Homeric parallels to Mark's gospel—parallels that even if not intended by the Markan evangelist might be identified by early Markan readers.

Fourth, MacDonald, though perhaps not intentionally so, has reopened a question that has long been neglected by Markan interpreters, namely the question of Markan source material. As noted in our introduction, the legacy of source, form, and redaction criticism has left this a forgotten issue in Markan studies. One error of source, form, and redaction criticism was to abandon the search for Mark's literary sources once it had been deduced that those sources did not include Matthew, Luke, or John. But MacDonald's work demonstrates that in light of ancient writing practices, Mark was not limited to the use of like genres or texts for his source material, but had the entire world of Jewish and Greco-Roman literature at his disposal. MacDonald's work also demonstrates that techniques and methods do exist to aid in the detection and identification of such sources.

For all of the above strengths (and perhaps many more unrecognized by this author), MacDonald's work is significant and must be taken seriously by Markan scholars and interpreters. It is however not without its weakness, an issue to which we now turn.

Weaknesses

Though MacDonald's work has many significant strengths and has made some significant contributions to both Markan and New Testament studies, it is not without its weaknesses. Here, we will identify and discuss those weaknesses.

The Primacy of Homer over the Jewish Scriptures

Our first critique of MacDonald's work is his claim that the Homeric epics are the *primary* literary model for Mark's narrative—primary even over Jewish scriptures. While MacDonald grants that Jewish scriptures certainly play a role in the composition of Mark's narrative, he ultimately concludes that this role is secondary to the role played by the Homeric epics.[7] This conclusion is suspect for many reasons. Jewish scriptures held significantly greater value in the life of the early church—the life out of which Mark's gospel presumably came—than the Homeric epics. In fact, there is much in the Homeric epics that would likely have been offensive to the sensibilities of the early church—a reality that should raise some questions about how significant a role it played in the composition of a gospel. Given these facts, *ceteris paribus*, Jewish scriptures provide a more likely literary influence for Mark's gospel than Homeric epics. Of course, MacDonald would not concede to all things being the same and would argue that Homeric material has a more dominant presence than material from Jewish scriptures. But how can such a claim be made? There is not a single quotation of Homeric material, but numerous quotations from Jewish scriptures—the gospel in fact begins with such a quotation. Not a single Homeric character appears in Mark's gospel, but numerous characters from Jewish scriptures appear. And while MacDonald is able to show some parallels between Markan pericopes and Homeric episodes, none of these parallels are as obvious or clear as parallels between Markan

---

7. MacDonald, *Homeric Epics*, 189.

pericopes and episodes from Jewish scriptures. In fact, at times, Jewish scriptures provide a more plausible parallel to a particular Markan pericope than the Homeric episode provided by MacDonald (as evidence we examine below will demonstrate). All of these reasons would indicate that Homeric primacy over Jewish scriptures was unlikely in the composition of Mark's gospel. This conclusion does not mean that Homeric epics did not serve as a literary model for Mark's gospel, but only that they did not serve as its *primary* model.

The Absence of Hypertextual Clues

One of the larger problems that MacDonald faces is the absence of clear hypertextual clues in Mark's gospel—clues to an author's use of a hypotext (imitated text) imbedded in the hypertext (imitating text). Perhaps most problematic is their absence at early stages in Mark's gospel. This absence is particularly problematic given that MacDonald concludes that the Markan evangelist intended his readers to identify and understand his transvaluation of the Homeric epics. But if this claim were true, one would expect to find specific and obvious clues at an early point in Mark's gospel—clues that would signal the reader to read with an eye on the episodes, characters, and themes of the Homeric epics. Such clues might include the name or description of a well known Homeric character, a direct quote from a Homeric episode, a pericope that strongly resembles a Homeric episode, or a unique Homeric detail or group of details. In MacDonald's case for Markan imitation of Homer, we find no such clues early in Mark's gospel. The first real Homeric parallel that MacDonald finds concerns Jesus' stilling of the storm in Mark 4:35–41. MacDonald argues that hypertextual clues exist, but that they are simply subtle. He argues that subtle imitation was quite common in the ancient world and that we should not be surprised to find it in Mark. MacDonald is certainly right that ancient authors often included subtle imitation, but he has not provided the whole truth. While subtle imitation can be found in many famous imitative works, Karl Olav Sandnes has noted that it is usually accompanied by more obvious imitation—imitation that will allow the reader the ability to decipher and appreciate the points of subtle imitation.[8] While the absence of these hypertextual clues does not rule out Markan imitation of Homer, it does raise questions about both the degree

---

8. Sandnes, "*Imitatio Homeri?*" 715–32.

of such imitation and also the evangelist's desire for readers to perceive such imitation.

Unpersuasive Similarities

In his attempt to demonstrate Mark's imitation of Homer, MacDonald draws up numerous similarities between the two texts. While some of these similarities are interesting and suggestive, many of them are relatively weak and ultimately unpersuasive. Here we will look at a two examples to demonstrate this weakness in MacDonald's work.

Sleeping Sailors: MacDonald draws a comparison between Mark's account of Jesus stilling a storm (Mark 4:35–41) and Homer's account of Odysseus' crew releasing the winds that had been given to Odysseus by Aeolus (10.1–69). For convenience, I provide here MacDonald's chart that lays out the similarities between these two texts.[9]

Odyssey 10.1–69	Mark 4:35–41
Odysseus' crew boarded and sat down. [recorded in 9.563–64]	Jesus boarded and sat down to teach [recorded in Mark 4:1–2]
On a floating island Odysseus told stories to Aeolus.	On a floating boat Jesus told his stories to the crowds. [recorded between Mark 4:1–33 presumably]
After a month he took his leave, boarded, and sailed with twelve ships.	When it was late, he took his leave, and sailed. "Other boats were with him."
Odysseus slept	Jesus slept
The greedy crew opened the sack of winds and created a storm: "All the winds rushed out."	A storm arose: "And there was a great gale of wind."
The crew groaned	The disciples were helpless and afraid
Odysseus awoke and gave up hope	Jesus awoke and stilled the storm
Odysseus complained of his crew's folly.	Jesus rebuked his disciples for lack of faith.
Aeolus was master of the winds.	Jesus was master of winds and sea.

At first glance, MacDonald's similarities seem impressive, and they fit his criteria of both density and sequence. But on closer examination, the similarities are not as strong as they appear.

---

9. For this chart, see MacDonald, *Homeric Epics*, 61.

Mark and Imitation

The first similarity compares Jesus boarding a boat and sitting with Odysseus' crew boarding a boat and sitting. But this similarity seems somewhat negligible as these actions would likely be present in any story that involved travel on a boat. And while both stories involve boarding and sitting on a boat, they are strikingly different in virtually all other details. Odysseus' crew is quickly boarding and sitting at the oars of the boat so that they can leave the island of the Cyclopes. Jesus boards and sits on a boat so that he can teach a large crowd. Aside from the two basic actions of boarding and sitting on a boat—presumably two very common actions in stories involving boats—these two elements have nothing in common, making the similarity quite weak.

The second similarity compares Odysseus' month long stay on the floating island of Aeolus the wind god with a scene in which Jesus teaches while seated in a boat. MacDonald highlights the following parallels: both Odysseus and Jesus are on objects floating in water (an island and a boat) and both are telling stories. But how legitimate and/or significant are these parallels? It seems quite a stretch to suggest that Jesus sitting in a boat is an intended imitation of Odysseus and his crew residing on the floating island of Aeolus for a month. The only similarity that exists is that each character is depicted as being on an object that happens to float (it should be noted that Mark never highlights the notion that the boat is "floating.") The claim that both Odysseus and Jesus are telling stories while on these floating objects also appears to be a forced similarity rather than a natural one. Odysseus recounts for Aeolus the events of his journey and the Trojan War. And though he is certainly portrayed as telling stories, the content of the stories are not given in the text. But Jesus is telling parables that instruct his audience about the Kingdom of God—parables for which the content is provided. To reduce this section in Mark's gospel to Jesus merely telling "stories" seems at best to be forcing an argument. Apart from these two suspect parallels, there is nothing else that would link Odysseus' stay on Aeolus' Island with Jesus' teaching parables from a boat.

The third similarity notes that both stories include the hero sailing with multiple boats—Mark noting the presence of other boats and Homer noting the presence of twelve boats. MacDonald thinks it odd that Mark would include the statement "other boats were with him." Perhaps such an inclusion is suspicious, but is it evidence of Mark imitating the Homeric detail of Odysseus traveling with twelve ships? Such imitation is possible, but other explanations could exist for this oddly placed detail.¹⁰

The fourth similarity notes that both Jesus and Odysseus are sleeping in the boat. Here it seems we have a legitimate point of contact between the two stories. However, we should note that this point of contact is not unique to these two stories alone. In fact, as many Markan interpreters note the character of Jonah found in Jewish scriptures also falls asleep in boat (Jonah 1:5).¹¹ While MacDonald has found a point of continuity between Mark and Homer, it is possible that a better point of continuity exists between Mark and Jewish scripture.

The fifth similarity notes the storm that comes upon the boat and its crew in both stories. Again there is a point of continuity between the stories. But again, this detail is not an uncommon one in the ancient world. It too finds a parallel in the story of Jonah (Jonah 1:4).

The sixth similarity compares the reactions of both Odysseus' crew and Jesus' disciples. But the only real similarity between the reactions of both groups is that they both have one. The only thing that Homer tells us about the reaction of Odysseus' crew—and he tells us only in a passing manner—is that they grieved or groaned as a result of their mistake and the storm that it caused. Mark's crew is described as being terrified by the storm and afraid for their lives. As a result, they approach Jesus for help. The response of Jesus' disciples and Odysseus' crew are more different than they are similar, making this proposed similarity quite weak. It should also be noted that the reaction of Jesus' disciples has more in common with the Jonah narrative than it does with this Homeric episode, i.e.,

---

10. Robert Gundry suggests that Mark includes this reference to other boats in order to demonstrate the large number of disciples Jesus had, i.e., there were more than twelve disciples following him and therefore additional boats were needed; *Apology for the Cross*, 238. Gerd Theissen has argued that Mark's story is a shortened version of a longer story in which the "other boats" were lost in the storm. Mark has then kept the detail of additional boats, but omitted their fate; *Miracle Stories*, 102, 180. G. Schille has argued that the presence of additional boats indicates a larger number of witnesses to the miracle than simply the twelve alone; "Die Seesturmerz hlungen Markus 4,35–51," 31. Adela Yarbro Collins argues that the entire story might be based on Psalms 107:23–32 (106:23–32 LXX), and that the presence of many boats would then reflect v. 23a "Those who go down to the sea in boats"; *Mark*, 258. Of all of these possibilities, this author feels all but the suggestion of Theissen are plausible explanations of this detail in Mark's gospel.

11. For examples, see Collins, *Mark*, 259–61; Guelich, *Mark*, 266; van Iersel, *Mark*, 194–96; Hooker, *St. Mark*, 138–39; et al.

both the crew in Jonah and Jesus' disciples are terrified by the storm and both awake a prophetic figure in order to seek his aid.

The seventh similarity compares the awakening and response to the storm of both Odysseus and Jesus—Odysseus loses hope and considers death, but Jesus calms the storm. Again there is a point of continuity here between these two stories. But again, the story of Jonah provides a more likely literary model for Mark. Jesus is awakened by his terrified disciples just as Jonah is awakened by the terrified crew. Odysseus, however, is presumably awoken by the storm alone, and certainly not by his crew. The responses of both men to the storm are also quite different. Odysseus considers giving up hope and jumping to his death in the sea, while Jesus successfully commands the winds and the waves to be still. Perhaps this is, as MacDonald claims, a Markan emulation and transvaluation of Odysseus, i.e., it presents Jesus as superior to Odysseus. But such a transvaluation only works if it can be shown that imitation exists between the two stories. The responses of both Odysseus and Jesus to the storm have no similarities other than they are both responses to a storm. There is nothing here to lead the reader to initially conclude that Markan imitation of Homer exists here.

The eighth similarity compares the reactions of Odysseus and Jesus to their followers. But again this similarity seems be a stretch. Jesus addresses his disciples, questioning their fear and lack of faith. But Odysseus never directly addresses his crew members or their failures. Odysseus only complains about his crew to Aeolus, when he returns to Aeolus' house to again ask for aid. It should be noted that these complaints only come after Odysseus and his crew have already set up camp and eaten together. Again, there are no true parallels between Jesus' reaction of to his disciples and Odysseus' reaction to his crew.

The ninth and final similarity compares Jesus as master of the winds and waves and Aeolus as the master of the wind and waves. This similarity is quite interesting, as both Homer and Mark present these respective characters as masters of the wind. But this similarity is not necessarily evidence of Markan imitation of Homer. It is a thematic similarity and one that could be easily explained by a Markan polemic against pagan beliefs. It is quite possible that Mark's story has an eye on Homer and the Homeric teachings regarding the source and origins of storms, i.e., they are stirred up by Greek gods and goddesses. But that Mark's gospel can be read as a response to Homeric claims is not evidence that Mark has used Homer as a literary model for imitation.

At the conclusion of our analysis, we find that only four of the nine similarities offered by MacDonald can be considered significant or substantial.

Odyssey 10.1–69	Mark 4:35–41
The presence of twelve boats	The presence of other boats
Odysseus falls asleep on the boat	Jesus falls asleep on the boat
A storm involving wind arises	A storm involving wind arises
Odysseus wakes up	Jesus is woken up

It must be noted that all but one of these details (the presence of other boats) in Mark find literary parallels in the story of Jonah, parallels that are actually closer to Mark than the parallels found in the *Odyssey*. We must also note that vast differences in the stories further obscure these few similarities. Ultimately, with regard to this Markan pericope, the evidence for Markan imitation of Homer appears weak.

Untriumphal Entries: MacDonald also argues that Mark's triumphal entry (Mark 11:1–14)—labeled by MacDonald as the untriumphal entry—imitates Odysseus' entry into the city of the Phaeacians (found in books 6 and 7). Again, MacDonald's chart that lays out the similarities between the two episodes has been provided.[12]

Odyssey 6 and 7	Mark 11:1–14
Odysseus arrived on the island of the Phaeacians bereft and unbefriended.	Jesus arrived in Judea without money or a host.
Athena told Nausicaa to ask her father for mules and a wagon.	Jesus told two of his disciples to find a colt and bring it to him.
Nausicaa told her father she needed the wagon to do her wash.	The disciples told those with the colt, "The Lord has need of it."

---

12. See MacDonald, *Homeric Epics*, 108–9.

Odyssey 6 and 7	Mark 11:1–14
Nausicaa went to the shore to wash clothing and there found Odysseus. "Folding the *clothes she packed them into her painted wagon*, hitched the sharp-hoofed *mules*, and *mounted the wagon*."	"They brought the *colt* to Jesus *and threw their cloaks on it*; and *he sat on it*.
Odysseus, though a king, entered the city wearing someone else's clothing, behind a mule wagon caring laundry.	Jesus, though Son of God, entered the city in humility, riding on someone else's beast of burden with clothing for a saddle.
Nausicaa thought Odysseus' coming was according to the will of the gods, and the Phaeacians thought he was divine.	The crowds shouted, "Blessed is he who comes in the name of the Lord"
He entered the city late in the day. "And there Odysseus stood, gazing at all this bounty" of glorious architecture and vegetation, including the fig trees that bore even out of season.	On entering the temple late in the day, Jesus "looked around at everything." The next day, he cursed a fig tree for bearing no fruit, even though "it was not the season for figs"

Again, there is a long list of similarities, and MacDonald claims they are both dense and sequential. But after further analysis, these similarities appear highly questionable.

The first similarity compares Odysseus arriving on the island of the Phaeacians with Jesus' arrival at Jerusalem. MacDonald notes that Odysseus was washed up on the island shore and that he was naked, hungry, and alone—perhaps at his greatest moment of need. He argues that similarly, Jesus arrives in Jerusalem without any money or a host—presumably also in need. MacDonald's description of the state in which Odysseus came to Phaeacia is accurate, but his description of the state in which Jesus came to Jerusalem is highly questionable. There is no indication in Mark's gospel that Jesus comes to Jerusalem without money or without a host. Perhaps MacDonald has assumed Jesus has no money or no host because he borrows a donkey from another person and because on the night of the last supper he must borrow a room in which to host the meal. But to discern from these two events that Jesus comes to Jerusalem without money or lodging is a significant leap in logic. In fact, the Markan text would indicate that Jesus had at least some lodging as he eats a meal while he is in Bethany (14:3–9). Here, MacDonald has created a similarity between Homer and Mark out of thin air, forcing the Markan text to say something that it clearly does not say. Therefore, no similarity actually exists.

The second similarity compares Athena directing Nausicaa to ask her father for mules and a wagon with Jesus directing his disciples to find him a colt. But when we look at this similarity, we find there is little similar between these two episodes. Athene appears to Nausicaa in a dream, at the same time taking the appearance of the daughter of Dymas. In the dream she scolds Nausicaa for being careless and not washing her fine clothes—clothes that will be needed when an appropriate suitor is chosen for her. In this dream, Athene instructs Nausicaa to, among other things, ask her father for mules and a wagon so she can take her laundry to be washed. Clearly, this interaction between Athene and Nausicaa has only one parallel with the episode of Mark's triumphal entry—the instruction to another/others to ask for an animal as a means for transportation. But here MacDonald has selected one very minor element of Athene's interaction with Nausicaa and used it as a basis for a central feature of Mark's triumphal entry pericope. It is highly questionable whether this similarity is distinct enough to make it a significant one, leaving interpreters hard pressed to accept this similarity as evidence of Mark's imitation of Homer.

The third similarity compares Nausicaa telling her father she needs mules and a wagon with the disciples telling the owner of the colt they have just untied, "The Lord has need of it." The way MacDonald presents this similarity is a bit misleading. Some readers may conclude that verbal agreement exists between these two attempts to procure an animal/animals, i.e., that both attempts verbally express the "need" for the animal/animals. No such agreement exists. Nausicaa's request never explicitly claims a "need" for the animals, though such need might be implicit. It should also be noted that Nausicaa explicitly asks her father for a wagon, but never explicitly for mules. The disciples never ask for the colt, but simply take it. It is only when they are asked why they are taking it that they explain that "The Lord has need of it." We must ask ourselves if a similarity even exists here, and if it does, is this similarity distinct enough to be considered significant? To many, this "similarity" will seem more likely to be coincidental than the result of Markan imitation of Homer.

The fourth similarity compares Nausicaa placing her clean and folded clothes in a wagon and then sitting in the wagon (not on the clothes) with Jesus placing clothes on a colt and then sitting on the colt. Again, this similarity hardly seems significant. Both stories do involve placing clothing on vessel of transportation and the subsequent sitting on that vessel, but the differences drastically obscure the similarities. The vessels of transportation are different (wagon vs. colt) and therefore, the clothes are placed on a different object. The characters doing the actions are in no way similar. The clothes are placed on the colt to serve as a saddle, while the clothes are placed on the wagon to be transported home. Nausicaa is returning home from doing her laundry, while Jesus is about to enter Jerusalem to kingly praise from a crowd. If MacDonald could show one or two more shared details, this similarity might be more compelling; but as it is, it is seems coincidental and insignificant—hardly strong evidence to suggest imitation on its own.

The fifth similarity compares Odysseus who enters the city in borrowed clothes and following a wagon drawn by mules with Jesus who enters a city on a borrowed mule while sitting on clothes. According to MacDonald, both characters enter the city in humility and in a manner that is unequal to their royal identity. Yet, again we must note that MacDonald's presentation of this similarity is misleading. Odysseus does not enter the city following a wagon pulled by mules. Rather, he follows the wagon until it comes near the city and then waits to enter the city alone at a later time. Therefore, the only real similarities are that both characters enter the city in a humble manner while possessing something borrowed. But again, the differences between these stories overshadow these minor similarities. Odysseus enters the cities of the Phaeacians secretly and is shrouded in a mist by the goddess Athene, while Jesus enters the city openly and publicly. In fact, in Mark's narrative, it seems like Jesus has purposely coordinated this event, so that it would be a public spectacle. When Odysseus enters the city he is met by no one except Athene who is disguised as a woman from the town. Jesus, however, is met by crowds of people who loudly proclaim his identity as king. While these respective accounts share a few minor details, they hardly resemble each other in any significant way, making it difficult to demonstrate a literary relationship between them.

The sixth similarity compares Nausicaa and the Phaeacians' belief that Odysseus had come to them by the will of the gods with the crowd's proclamation that Jesus had come in the name of the Lord. But again what MacDonald suggests is a similarity does not in fact appear to be one. These two narrative elements are different both in the way they are expressed and in their substance. These two elements have no similarities in there narrative expression. Nausicaa and the Phaeacians' beliefs about the nature of Odysseus' arrival are mentioned in passing and privately. Ultimately, they play a minor role in the narrative. In contrast, the crowd's proclamation in Mark are public and prominent in the narrative. Ultimately, they play a significant role in the narrative. These two beliefs are also different in their substance. The belief expressed in the *Odyssey* is simply regarding the will of the gods, i.e., the gods have orchestrated the events that brought Odysseus to the Phaeacians. But the belief expressed in Mark is regarding the identity of Jesus, i.e., Jesus is the messianic king and ancestor of David who comes in the name of the Lord. Again we find that this suggested similarity, if it can even be regarded as such, is a weak one and cannot be taken as significant evidence of imitation.

The seventh similarity compares Odysseus observing the beautiful bounty and architecture of the palace of Alcinous—bounty that includes trees that bear figs even out of season—with Jesus observing the temple and later cursing a fig tree that did not bear figs out of season. But the similarities between Jesus observing the Jewish temple and Odysseus observing the Alcinous' palace are hardly compelling. Odysseus' observation is described in great detail and the things he sees are numerous (e.g., golden doors, silver pillars, its immortal occupants, fine-spun delicate cloths, fifty serving women, and fruit trees that are continually in season). But Mark offers no description of what Jesus' sees when he enters the temple. It is two chapters later when the disciples admire the large stones and buildings in the temple court. But even these comments, hardly compare to Odysseus' observation of Alcinous' palace.

At first glance, the fact that both Mark and Homer make reference to fig trees bearing fruit out of season appears to be a compelling similarity—more compelling than any similarity between these episodes that we have noted to this point. But the significance of this similarity is mitigated somewhat when we consider that in Odysseus' observation, he specifically notes an orchard in which all the trees constantly bear fruit. The list of fruits from the orchard is long, and it happens to include figs. It is possible that this reference to fruit trees that continually produce fruit regardless of the season has influenced Mark's reference to the unproductive frig tree. However, such a conclusion is far from certain. It is quite possible that both stories are reflecting a common motif in the ancient world of divine blessing. Ultimately, while this similarity is suggestive, on its own, it does not demonstrate Markan imitation of Homer.

In this attempt to show Markan imitation of Homer, MacDonald has strung together a number of vague, minor, and at times misleading similarities. Virtually all of these similarities lack distinction, making any claim to density of similarities and sequence of similarities irrelevant. Ultimately, Mark's triumphal entry pericope shares virtually no significant similarities with Homer's episode of Odysseus entering Phaeacia. Therefore, one is ultimately left to conclude that literary dependence is unlikely.

These two examples of MacDonald's analysis are representative of a significant amount of the analysis found throughout MacDonald's work. At times, MacDonald is able to offer similarities that seem stronger and more significant than those we have critiqued here. A handful of similarities are even quite suggestive of some relationship between Mark and Homer, though perhaps not one as broad as MacDonald has suggested. But on the whole, too many of the similarities MacDonald proposes are overly vague, lacking in distinction, minor in character, and undermined by significant narrative differences.

Evidence: Subtle and Suggestive vs. Clear and Obvious

Perhaps the most significant problem in MacDonald's work is that his best evidence is subtle and at best suggestive of Markan imitation of Homer. MacDonald is unable to provide a single example of clear and obvious Markan imitation of Homer. By clear and obvious, I mean an example where the narrative details (characters, actions, objects, etc.) and narrative sequence are so similar that Markan imitation of Homer is difficult to deny or doubt. Many examples of such clear and obvious imitation can be found above in our comparison of Homer and Virgil. If MacDonald could produce just one example in which Mark has clearly imitated Homer, it would strengthen the entirety of his work. The subtle and suggestive evidence that he has put forth would be significantly reinforced and much easier to accept. However, until an example of such imitation can be provided, MacDonald's work will remain what it is, namely a fresh, provocative, and suggestive of a possible literary relationship between Mark and the Homeric epics. Yet, because MacDonald's evidence is at best suggestive, it will ultimately convince few.

MOVING FORWARD WITH MARK AND IMITATION

Our evaluation of MacDonald's work has provided a number of considerations that influence our present study of Mark and imitation. First, in identifying literary models for Mark, primary consideration should be given to Jewish scriptures or religious texts rather than Greco-Roman literature. As we have noted, Mark's gospel clearly expresses the value it places on Jewish scripture, and such texts are presumably much closer to the evangelist's world view and commitments than pagan Greco-Roman texts. Second, the Markan text should contain clear and obvious clues to any text that is proposed as a significant literary model. Examples of such clues might include quoting of the imitated text, referring to a character from the imitating text, or the presence of events or details that strongly parallel events or details in the imitating text. Such markers do not prove imitation has taken place, but without them imitation becomes less plausible and more difficult to demonstrate. Third, noted similarities between the imitating text and the imitated text need to be, on the whole, distinctive and significant. Certainly, there may be times when similarities are subtle or perhaps vague, as such imitation was at times used by ancient authors. But subtle and vague similarities, if not accompanied by distinct and significant similarities, provide a weak basis for demonstrating imitation.

3

Mark and the Elijah-Elisha Narrative

INTRODUCTION

INTERPRETERS HAVE CERTAINLY RECOGNIZED a relationship between Mark's Gospel and the Elijah-Elisha narrative of 1 and 2 Kings.[1] But on the nature and extent of this relationship, interpreters' conclusions vary. Many readily acknowledge the miracles of Elijah and Elisha as patterns for the Markan miracle stories, e.g., the healing of a leper, the raising of a dead child, or the multiplication of loaves. Parallels between Mark's presentation of Elijah and John the Baptist are also frequently noted. However, most interpreters relegate the relationship between Mark and the Elijah-Elisha narrative to the micro level (seeing the Elijah-Elisha narrative as a background or pattern for this particular Markan detail or that Markan pericope) and completely ignore the possibility of a relationship at the macro level (seeing the Elijah-Elisha narrative as a literary pattern or source for the entire Markan narrative).

The one notable exception to this minimizing tendency is the work of Wolfgang Roth, *Hebrew Gospel: Cracking the Code of Mark*, a work that has received relatively little attention from subsequent Markan commentators.[2] Here, we will summarize and analyze Roth's work. Ultimately,

---

1. For examples, see Guillaume, Miraculously Repeated," 21–23; Pagliara, *La figura di Elia*; Dautzenberg, "Elija im Markusevangelium," 1077–94; Miller and Miller, *The Gospel of Mark as Midrash*; van Iersel, *Mark*, 63–66, 102, 127–34; Marcus, *Mark*, 156–58, 181–86; Collins, *Mark*, 28–29, 157. For scholars who note similarities between the Elijah-Elisha narrative and the canonical gospels (not specifically Mark), see Lindars, "Elijah, Elisha," 63–79; Aune, *Literary Environment*, 40–41; and Brown, "Jesus and Elisha," 85–104. As noted in our introduction, this narrative begins in 1 Kings 16:29 and end with 2 Kings 13:25.

2. Roth, *Hebrew Gospel*.

this analysis will aid us in moving forward with our own investigation of Mark's possible use of the Elijah-Elisha narrative.

WOLFGANG ROTH'S *HEBREW GOSPEL*: A SUMMARY

Roth's ultimate argument is that the entire Gospel of Mark is patterned after the Elijah-Elisha narrative of 1 and 2 Kings. His basic starting point is the close association in Mark between John the Baptist and Elijah. In light of this association, he argues that Mark presents Jesus as Elisha. For Roth, Jesus' baptism by John parallels Elijah's ascension into heaven. As Elisha receives a double portion of Elijah's spirit (presumably the Holy Spirt), Jesus receives the Holy Spirit at the point of John's baptism. With this starting point, Roth goes on to provide a number of various evidences that he believes demonstrate Mark's dependence on the Elijah-Elisha narrative.

He begins by providing seven Markan passages/features he believes are patterned after the Elijah-Elisha narrative, suggesting therefore that the former used the latter as a literary model. First, he notes that both the Markan Jesus and Elisha do the same number of miracles—that is if one counts Jesus' miracles from the beginning of Mark's gospel to Mark 7:37 (at which point the people state, "He has done everything well; he even makes the deaf to hear and the mute to speak."). Second, he argues that Mark's link between John's baptism of Jesus and Jesus' cleansing of the temple—a link reflected in Mark 11:27–33—parallels the Elijah-Elisha narrative's link between Elijah commissioning of Elisha and the purification of the temple by Joash. He argues that John's baptism of Jesus and Elijah's commissioning of Elisha are both seminal events for the temple cleansings that eventually follow them. Third, Roth argues that both the Markan Jesus' ministry and Elisha's ministry begin after the completion of their predecessor's ministries. In addition, both the ministry of Elisha and the ministry of Jesus aim to establish God's divine rule. Fourth, Roth argues that the parable of the four soils finds parallels in the Elijah-Elisha narrative. The number one hundred used to describe the uppermost yield of the good seed in Mark is a number that also occurs twice in the Elijah-Elisha narrative in association with the results of righteous behavior (1 Kgs 18:4, 13; 2 Kgs 4:43). Furthermore, the Elijah-Elisha narrative also provides parallels to the three bad soils in Mark's parable: (1) the seed fallen on the path parallels Jezebel who immediately rejects the prophets of God; (2) the seed fallen on rocky ground parallels Ahab who first obeys but then disobeys the prophets of God; and (3) the seed fallen among the weeds parallels Jehoram who first responds positively to God but eventually responds negatively. Fifth, Roth argues that Mark begins his gospel with the ministry of John the Baptist because he is constrained by an Elijah-John the Baptist comparison, i.e., because the Elijah-Elisha narrative begins with Elijah's ministry, Mark must begin with John's ministry. The inclusion of a birth narrative of some sort would violate Mark's use of the Elijah-Elisha narrative. Sixth, Roth argues that Mark's doubling of the feeding narrative (the feeding of both 5,000 and 4,000) parallels a feature in the Elijah-Elisha narrative, namely the tendency for Elisha to duplicate the miracles of Elijah. Not only does Elisha duplicate some of Elijah's miracles, but he doubles the total number of Elijah's miracles—from eight to sixteen. Roth also notes that in the same way Elisha does eight more miracles than Elijah, the Markan Jesus does eight more miracles than Elisha.[3] Seventh, Roth argues that Peter's triple denial of Jesus (Mark 14:66–72) parallels Elisha's triple refusal to leave Elijah before his ascension (2 Kings 2:1–12). Roth concludes that these seven examples all affirm the conclusion that Mark is using the Elijah-Elisha narrative as a literary model. The rest of his book seeks to demonstrate how other parallels between Mark and the Elijah-Elisha narrative support this hypothesis.

The parallels between Mark and the Elijah-Elisha narrative provided by Roth are both diverse and numerous. He begins by noting structural similarities between the two narratives, as well as shared spatial similarities. Regarding structural similarities, he argues that both narratives can be divided into four acts. Regarding similarities in spatial orientation, he argues that both narratives begin in the Transjordan, and that both have decisive confrontations in urban royal centers. In addition to these similarities, Roth argues that similar forms of narration exist in both narratives. Two examples can be given. One, both narratives have series of independent and subordinate scenes. That is to say, both narratives contain a mixture of long chains of independent scenes that could stand on their own as well as long chains of subordinate stories that only make sense in

---

3. However, Roth's count of these eight miracles of Jesus—beyond the first sixteen that parallel the total number of Elisha' miracles—is relatively subjective. His list includes Jesus' cleansing of the temple and the tearing of the temple veil—both events that are questionably identified as miracles performed by Jesus. See Roth, *Hebrew Gospel*, 16.

the contextual chain. Two, both narratives also have similar scene types, including dialog narratives, vision audition stories, and action episodes.

Roth then turns to a litany of specific details (e.g., words, phrases, numbers, etc.) that are shared by both Mark and the Elijah-Elisha narrative; details that he believes demonstrate the former's literary dependence on the latter. Here we will provide a number of examples. He suggests that Judas' kiss of betrayal in Mark parallels the remnant of 7,000 in 1 Kings 19 who have refused to betray Yahweh by kissing Baal (1 Kgs 19:18). He argues that Jesus' identification of Gentiles with dogs (Mark 7:24–30) could find its literary origin in Hazael's self-identification as a dog (2 Kgs 8:13). He notes that Jesus' charge to the rich man to "Go, sell what you own and give the money to the poor" (Mark 10:21), finds a parallel in Elisha's instruction to the widow: "Go sell the oil and pay your debts" (2 Kgs 4:7). For Roth, Jesus' forty days in the wilderness (Mark 1:12–13) closely resembles the forty days that Elijah spent in the wilderness (1 Kgs 19:1–7). In both accounts, the central character is attended to by angels! According to Roth, Jesus' specific instruction to his disciples not to take with them money or two cloaks (Mark 6:8–9) finds a unique parallel in Gehazi's misguided request from Naaman for silver and two cloaks (2 Kgs 5:22).

After demonstrating numerous shared details between Mark and the Elijah-Elisha narrative, Roth presents similar narrative plots that appear in both narratives. He compares the Markan account of Jesus healing a paralytic to the Elijah-Elisha narrative's account of King Ahaziah falling from roof. While the Markan account presents a man lowered through a roof while lying on a mat, the 2 Kings account presents a man who falls from a roof resulting in confinement to his bed. The Markan account ends in a healing brought about by faith, while the 2 Kings account ends in death brought about by apostasy. He also demonstrates that both Mark and the Elijah-Elisha narrative contain stories of temple restorations. In Mark, Jesus cleanses the temple by overturning the money changers' tables. In the Elijah-Elisha narrative, the priest Jehoiada cleanses the local Baal sanctuary by killing its priest and tearing down its altars (2 Kings 11:17–18). He also compares the martyrdom of Jesus with the martyrdom of Naboth. Both narratives include (among other things) false accusations, jealous/threatened leaders of Israel, and the death of a righteous figure.

It is with these last considerations that Roth concludes his case for Mark's dependence on the Elijah-Elisha narrative as a literary model. His work concludes with two chapters that consider the hermeneutical activity of the evangelist that led to the final form of the second gospel as well as literary analogies for the types of literary dependence Roth believes he has demonstrated. With regard to the issue of literary analogies, Roth notes both Haggadic midrash and Greco-Roman imitation.

WOLFGANG ROTH'S *HEBREW GOSPEL*: AN EVALUATION

Strengths

Roth's work has two strengths that should be noted. First, his work is one of the first studies to consider a relationship between Mark and the Elijah-Elisha narrative on the macro level. As we stated in our introduction, many scholars have noted Mark's use of the Elijah-Elisha narrative on the mirco level, i.e., as a likely background for this Markan detail or that Markan pericope. But the abundance of connections between Mark and the Elijah-Elisha narrative at the micro level strongly suggests that a relationship on the macro level also exists. Roth has taken this suggestion seriously, and his exploration of this suggestion has yielded results that other Markan interpreters have missed or ignored.

Second, Roth's work has provided many significant and insightful similarities between Mark and the Elijah-Elisha narrative—similarities that should not be ignored by Markan interpreters. The similarity between Jesus' and Elijah's wilderness experiences, though it has been noted by some scholars, seems more significant than has previously been recognized. Jesus' instruction to his disciples regarding what to take with them as they travel finds a striking similarity in the story of Gehazi, Elisha's disciple. Similarities between Jesus and Naboth also deserve further consideration, especially in light of the parable of the wicked tenants, which like the Naboth story includes both a vineyard and the murder of an innocent man. Similarities between Jesus' and Elisha's healing of a leper are also noteworthy. These and other similarities noted by Roth are a great strength of his work, and open the door for further investigation of the relationship between Mark's gospel and the Elijah-Elisha narrative.

Weaknesses

While Roth's work offers some significant contributions to the field of Markan studies, it also has numerous weaknesses—weaknesses that are likely responsible for the general scholarly neglect the work has experienced. Perhaps the most significant weaknesses in Roth's work are related to his method and approach to determining literary dependence. Roth neither establishes criteria for determining literary dependence, nor provides for his readers any example of what literary dependence in the Greco-Roman world might look like. As a result, there is no means for evaluating whether the evidence Roth puts forth actually demonstrates literary dependence. In a way, Roth takes a "shotgun" approach, placing before the reader numerous and wide-ranging evidences and hoping that the magnitude of the blast will be convincing. But because Roth has failed to provide any means of detecting or evaluating evidence for literary dependence, the reader is left to question whether Roth has actually met his burden of proof.

Another methodological problem is that Roth begins his work with a particular premise regarding Mark's intention (that Mark has patterned the characters of John the Baptist and Jesus after Elijah and Elisha, respectively), a premise that supports his ultimate conclusion that Mark's gospel is dependent on the Elijah-Elisha narrative as a literary model. He then reads both Mark and the Elijah-Elisha narrative in light of that premise and conclusion. The problems with this approach should be quite clear. First, the work as whole largely rests on the validity of the original premise—a premise that we will soon demonstrate is quite weak. If the premise is undermined, much of the work collapses. Second, because the author approaches Mark and the Elijah-Elisha narrative with the presumption of literary dependence, his interpretation of the evidence is often forced or arbitrary. A better approach would be to begin with realities in the text and then, if literary dependence could be demonstrated, provide theories regarding the author's intertextual intentions.

Another weakness concerns the author's original premise that was noted above, namely that the Markan evangelist has strictly patterned his presentation of John the Baptist and Jesus on the characters of Elijah and Elisha, respectively. But after careful examination of the Markan text, such rigid associations fall apart. While it is true that Mark clearly identifies John the Baptist with the eschatological Elijah (particularly through Jesus' clear statement linking the two figures, Mark 9:13), he does not restrict Elijah imagery to his depiction of John the Baptist alone. Such imagery is also applied to Jesus by the Markan evangelist. While Jesus is in the wilderness he is in the presence of wild animals and attended to by angels—

Mark and the Elijah-Elisha Narrative

a parallel to Elijah's (not Elisha's) wilderness experiences where he is fed by birds and attended to by angels. Also Jesus' calling of disciples has closer parallels to Elijah than to Elisha—who himself is a called disciple rather than one who calls disciples. While more of Jesus' miracles find parallels with those of Elisha, parallels with Elijah's miracles also exist (e.g., raising the dead [cf. 1 Kings 17:17–24] and walking on water [cf. 2 Kings 2:8]). It is perhaps most important to note that while the characters of Mark's gospel identify Jesus with Elijah or one of the prophets (perhaps Elisha; cf. Mk 6:15; 8:28), the evangelist clearly rejects such identities. Ultimately, the premise that Roth has based his study on has significant weaknesses and is untenable.

Another weakness in Roth's work concerns the quality of evidence Roth is able to provide. When closely examined, some of Roth's evidence is quite weak and ultimately proves little. Here a number of examples are provided. Roth claims that the total number of miracles that Jesus does in the gospel up until verse 7:37 matches the total number of miracles that Elisha does; both do sixteen. But the establishment of verse 7:37 as a stopping point for counting Jesus' miracles seems quite arbitrary. It is true that the people say of Jesus "He has done everything well," but there is nothing implicit or explicit that tells the reader they should take note of the total number of miracles to this point, or that the total number of miracles to this point has any significance (e.g., that it parallels the total of miracles performed by Elisha). Six more miracles come after this point in the narrative, making Jesus' total number of miracles twenty-two. Therefore, without Roth's arbitrary stopping point at verse 7:37, the proposed similarity between Jesus and Elijah disappears.

Roth also argues that both Mark and the Elijah-Elisha narrative are broken up into four acts. But the four acts he proposes for Mark seem arbitrary, and they are hardly recognized by the majority of Markan commentators.[4] He suggests that Mark's first act covers 1:1–13; yet this section seems to function as a prologue rather than the first "act" of the narrative.[5]

---

4. For a variety of different structures suggested for Mark's gospel, none of which agree with Roth, see the following: Pesch, *Naherwartungen*, 50–73; Guelich, *Mark*, xxxvii; Donahue and Harrington, *Gospel of Mark*, 46–50; France, *Gospel of Mark*, 11–15; Stein, *Mark*, 35–37; van Iersel, *Mark*, 18–26; Boring, *Mark*, 4–6. Morna Hooker's words regarding attempts to discern Mark's structure are particularly relevant here: "This means that we must recognize that any attempt to analyse the gospel is bound to be arbitrary, since we are imposing our own pattern on the material." Hooker, *Mark*, 16.

5. For such a conclusion, see France, *Mark*, 11–15; Moloney, *Gospel of Mark*, 20–21; Donahue and Harrington, *Mark*, 46–50; Boring, *Mark*, 4–6.

Similarly, Mark 16:1–8 might also be better identified as an epilogue rather than as a final fourth act.[6] Equating this first Markan act to the first act in the Elijah-Elisha narrative is also problematic, since the former covers only thirteen verse, while the latter covers over six chapters! Ultimately, Roth's argument that both Mark and the Elijah-Elisha narrative share a four act structure is weak evidence for literary dependence.

Another weakness concerns the numerous shared details that Roth finds between Mark's gospel and the Elijah-Elisha narrative. Many of these shared details are minor and are better explained as coincidental rather than evidence of literary dependence. A good example is Roth's claim that Mark has borrowed Judas' kiss of betrayal from the description in 1 Kings of the faithful remnant who had not kissed Baal. The only detail these narratives actually share is the mention of a kiss. Such a similarity could be found between Mark and any number of ancient texts.[7] If such a shared detail even needs an explanation, common coincidence seems preferred to literary dependence.

An additionally example is Roth's claim that Jesus' calling of the first four disciples (Mark 1:16–20) is patterned after the four lepers who proclaim God's miraculous defeat of the Arameans (2 Kings 7:3–16). But again, the only actual similarity between these two stories is the presence of four men. The four disciples in Mark have nothing in common with the four lepers in the Elijah-Elisha narrative apart the very general similarity that both groups will bear a message of good news. To draw these two stories together on such slight evidence seems to be exploiting a narrative coincidence.

A final example is Roth's claim that Jesus' order to the rich man to "go sell" his possessions and give them to the poor is modelled after Elisha's instructions to a widow to "go sell" her oil to pay back her creditor and support herself and her son. But these stories have no similarities other than the instruction to "go sell," And even this one similarity lacks verbal agreement, as Mark uses different words than the Elijah-Elisha narrative to convey the order. The complete lack of verbal agreement is certainly surprising if Mark is indeed dependent on the Elijah-Elisha narrative.

---

6. This conclusion is offered by Moloney, *Mark*, 20–21.

7. The verb καταφιλέω, "to kiss" is used twenty times in the Old Testament and Apocrypha. Once the word is even used to describe David kissing his son Absalom who would go on to betray him (2 Sam 14:33). If a background from Jewish scriptures is needed, this text seems like a much better choice than the passage suggested by Roth.

Again, if this similarity even needs explanation, a common coincidence seems to be most likely one.

While not all of Roth's evidence is so easily disregarded, much of it needs further development and substantiation. For example, the parallels between Mark's Jesus and Naboth, which we noted above, are interesting and suggestive, but more work needs to be done to demonstrate literary dependence and the nature of that dependence. Likewise, the similarity between Jesus' instruction to his disciples regarding money and clothing and Elisha's disciple Gehazi taking money and clothing seems unique and suggestive; but more thorough analysis is needed to demonstrate literary dependence. One or two shared details between two narrative episodes are intriguing, but because they can often be explained as coincidental, they cannot demonstrate literary dependence on their own. Too often, Roth's presentation of evidence is cursory and in need of further development.

A final weakness with Roth's work is his underlying assumption that Markan literary dependence on the Elijah-Elisha narrative is directly related to the ultimate narrative purposes of the Markan evangelist. Because Roth sees the Elijah-Elisha narrative as a major source for Mark's gospel, he concludes that the former must be an interpretive key for the latter. As a result, Roth concludes that Mark is presenting Jesus as a second Elisha whose aim is to restore the reign of God over Israel. But Roth's assumption here is misguided. While an author's source material may directly reflect the author's narrative purposes, it does not necessarily do so. In the Greco-Roman practice of imitation, the goal was not always to comment on the imitated work or to bring the meaning of the imitated work to bear on the imitating work. Often the goal of imitation was to preserve elements of the past in the writing of the present. At other times, imitation was simply a standard means or technique of writing. We cannot assume that in imitating another text an author intended to bring the full meaning or purposes of the imitated text to the imitating text.

MOVING BEYOND ROTH IN THE PRESENT STUDY

Roth has provided a provocative study, but as our evaluation has demonstrated, it is at best an initial first step in exploring Mark's use of the Elijah-Elisha narrative. To establish such dependence, a better methodology is needed. Consideration for how ancient authors used other texts is necessary, as are set criteria for establishing literary dependence.

The present study has accomplished both of these things in chapter one. In addition, much of Roth's evidence needs to be developed further in order for it to be useful in demonstrating Mark's use of 1 and 2 Kings. The present study will not only develop some of the evidence and arguments found in Roth's work, but more importantly, it will also consider new evidence indicating Mark's dependence on the Elijah-Elisha narrative. Finally, the present work will not assume that Markan dependence on the Elijah-Elisha narrative is evidence for Mark's narrative, theological, or rhetorical purposes. The purpose of this work is to simply establish whether literary dependence exists, leaving the question of the significance of that dependence for another day.

4

General Similarities between Mark and the Elijah-Elisha Narrative

INTRODUCTION

Before we begin to look at particular Markan texts and their possible relationship to the Elijah-Elisha narrative, we will consider a number of general similarities between the two narratives. These general similarities include genre, narrative length, episodic style, and geographical structure.[1] In considering these similarities between Mark and the Elijah-Elisha narrative, we seek to demonstrate the following: (1) that certain similarities increase the plausibility that the Markan evangelist is using the Elijah-Elisha narrative as a source; and (2) that certain similarities are easily—and perhaps best—explained by the theory that the Markan evangelist used the Elijah-Elisha narrative as a source.

GENRE

The genre of Mark's gospel (as well as the genre of all the canonical gospels) has long been debated. For the larger part of the twentieth century, the majority of gospel scholars regarded the canonical gospel as a new type/genre of literature, having no precedent in the ancient world.[2] However, in the last several decades an increased respect for the gospels as literature and an increased appreciation for literary theory have caused this

---

1. Here we must note that in regard to these similarities this study is indebted to the work of Thomas Brodie who has addressed them in his work *The Crucial Bridge*, 86–95 (republished in *The Birthing of the New Testament*, 147–53). However, we have expanded on Brodie's work, including original evidence and considerations.

2. This position was championed in large part by form critics including R. Bultmann, M. Dibelius, and K. L. Schmidt.

position to wane. It has been recognized that for the gospels to have been understood in the ancient world, they would have had to be related to the literary conventions and genres of that world. The ancient genre that has drawn the most significant comparisons to the canonical gospels is that of Greco-Roman βίοι, or ancient biography.³ But while many scholars are recognizing a relationship between the gospels and ancient biography, the nature and extent of the relationship is uncertain. Part of the problem lies in the vast varieties of biography that existed in the ancient world, as well as the lack of scholarly agreement regarding the classification of these different varieties.⁴ While Mark's gospel might share an affinity with one type of biography, it might lack affinity with one or two other types. What is generally concluded, therefore, is that in broad terms Mark falls into the category of ancient biography, but that it has combined other types of writing with biography, resulting in a unique form of ancient βίοι.

One such type of writing that Mark seems to have combined with the form of ancient biography is that of history or historiography. Adela Yarbro Collins has argued that while the primary content of Mark's gospel is the life of Jesus, its primary concern is not the life of Jesus in and of itself, but rather the life of Jesus as it relates to the unfolding of God's divine plan in the history of Israel and the world—a plan in which Jesus certainly plays a highly significant role. Jesus is the messianic agent of God whose actions and teachings are bringing about God's Kingdom and establishing it over the kingdoms of the world.⁵ Therefore, the biographical information about Jesus serves a historical purpose in a sense.⁶ Because for Mark

---

3. It should be noted that even in the first half of the twentieth century—the heyday of form criticism—a handful of scholars were exploring the connection between the canonical gospels and anicent Greco-Roman biography, e.g., Weiss, *Das Älteste Evangelium*; and Votaw, "Contemporary Biographies," 45–73, 217–49. The resurrection of such comparisons can primarily be attributed to Talbert, *What is a Gospel?* Later noteworthy studies include, Burridge, *What are the Gospels?*; Dormeyer, *Das Markusevangelium als Idealbiographie*; and Aune, *Literary Environment*.

4. See the differences between the classifications of ancient biography in the following works; Leo, *Die griechisch-römische Biographie*; Momigliano, *Development of Greek Biography*, Talbert, *What is a Gospel?*; Collins, *Mark*, 22–33.

5. For discussion on Mark as a promotion of Jesus and God's Kingdom over earthly rulers and Kingdoms, see Evans, "The Beginning of the Good News", 83–103; Incigneri, *Gospel to the Romans*; Winn, *Purpose of Mark's Gospel*.

6. The word "historical" should not be understood in the modern positivistic sense, which is overly concerned with accurately transmitting historical data, but rather in the ancient sense, which was concerned with a representational or explanatory transmission

General Similarities between Mark and the Elijah-Elisha Narrative

and the early church this action of God—through the agency of Jesus—marks the end (or impending end) of the present age, the gospel also takes on an eschatological dimension, one that at certain points is expressed in apocalyptic terms and imagery. Both this eschatological dimension and its apocalyptic expression are foreign to the genre of ancient biography, and so have been uniquely combined with it by the Markan evangelist.

Therefore, Mark might best be identified as an eschatological historical biography.[7] But while this description of Mark's genre may establish it as a unique biographical form in the larger genre of ancient Greco-Roman biography, it is not entirely without a parallel in the ancient world. Here we turn to the Elijah-Elisha narrative of 1 and 2 Kings—a text that comes from the sacred scriptures of the Markan evangelist—in order to see if it might provide a possible pattern for Mark's distinct combination of literary types.

On the surface, the Elijah-Elisha narrative appears to fall into the genre of history or historiography. It records the history of the northern (and to some degree southern) kingdom of Israel—including monarchial successions, military exploits, and diplomatic relations. But interestingly, biographical information is the primary vehicle that drives the historical purpose of the narrative. At the heart of the history are the prophets Elijah and Elisha—two figures whose activities and accomplishments dominate approximately seventy percent of the narrative. We must also note that the history that is being advanced in the narrative is not secular history, but religious history. It is a historical account of how God's divine plan—the elimination of idolatry and the restoration of the temple—is accomplished through his divine prophetic agents, Elijah and Elisha. Therefore, in the Elijah-Elisha narrative of 1 and 2 Kings, biographical information is the primary means of communicating God's activity in Israel's history.

We therefore see a distinct parallel between the genre of Mark's gospel and the genre of the Elijah-Elisha narrative. Both are to a certain degree a combination of biography and historiography. In the Elijah-Elisha narrative, the history of God's divine plan is told primarily through the

---

of historical data. For an excellent discussion on the ancient notion of history as it relates to Mark's gospel, see Collins, *Mark*, 33–42.

7. Collins opts for the label "Eschatological Historical Monograph" (*Mark*, 42), though it is difficult to understand why she has substituted "Monograph" for "Biography" when in her discussion of genre she demonstrates such close affinity between Mark and two different types of ancient biography.

biographical accounts of God's prophetic agents. In the Gospel of Mark, a biography of Jesus is used in order to communicate Jesus' identity and role (that of God's Son and final agent) in the historical unfolding of God's divine plan. While the primary generic identity of both narratives differ (Mark's being biography and the Elijah-Elisha narrative's being historiography), the combination of the same two generic types in both narratives raises the possibility that Mark's unique form of ancient Greco-Roman biography has been influence by (or perhaps patterned after?) the Elijah-Elisha narrative's form of historiography.

The other notable difference between the genre of Mark's gospel and that of the Elijah-Elisha narrative is the presence of eschatological and apocalyptic elements that are present in the former and absent in the latter. But this difference is not a difficult one and can easily be explained by the historical setting and circumstances of both narratives. Whether 1 and 2 Kings was composed in pre-exilic or exilic period, its composition took place a significant period of time before eschatological (or apocalyptic) expectations had widely influenced Israel's religious traditions. In contrast, Mark's gospel was written at a time when eschatological expectations/tensions were high, and the apocalyptic expressions of those expectations were common. Therefore, that we find eschatological and apocalyptic elements in Mark's gospel and not in the Elijah-Elisha narrative is not surprising.

OVERALL LENGTH

Relatively little attention has been paid to Mark's overall length and any significance that length may have.[8] Because the interpretive pay-off of Mark's length is likely perceived by many as slight, this lack of attention is not surprising. But when considering Mark's relationship to other ancient literature, Mark's length should play some role.[9]

Mark's gospel is 11,242 words long,[10] placing it within the parameters that Richard Burridge ascribes to ancient biographies—a genre of "medium" length (10,000 to 25,000 words).[11] Examples of biographies that are of similar length to Mark include Plutarch's *Parallel Lives*, averag-

---

8. For an exception, see Burridge, *What are Gospels*, 199–200.
9. See Brodie, *Crucial Bridge*, 88; idem, *Birthing*, 150.
10. See Morgenthaler, *Statistik des neutestamentlichen Wortschatzes*, Table 3, 164.
11. See Burridge, *What are Gospels*, 117–19, 168–69, 199–200.

General Similarities between Mark and the Elijah-Elisha Narrative

ing around 10,000 to 11,000 words, and Suetonius' *Lives of the Caesars*, averaging around 10,000 words.[12] But it must be noted that this category of a "medium" length literary work is quite broad, with some examples falling even outside Burridge's suggested range, e.g., Philo's *Life of Moses* (c. 32,000 words), Philostratus' *Apollonius of Tyana* (c. 82,000 words), and Lucian's *Demonax* (c. 3,000 words).[13] Why then is Mark's gospel the length that it is? Both of the other synoptic gospels are much larger, with Matthew at 18,305 words and Luke at 19,428 words.[14] Answering this question with any certainty is likely not possible. The answer may simply be that Mark recorded the material he had and was not limited or constrained by any discernible outside factors. But here we would like to raise the possibility that Mark's length might be influenced by the Elijah-Elisha narrative. The narrative is approximately 14,400 words—only about 3,000 words longer than Mark's gospel.[15] These two narratives are therefore quite similar with regard to their length. It is not implausible then that the length of the Elijah-Elisha narrative could have served as a general guideline for the Markan evangelist.

Clearly the similarity of length proves nothing in and of itself regarding a relationship between Mark's gospel and the Elijah-Elisha narrative. Many other factors could have played a role in Mark's length. But the similarity in length along with the genre similarities enhances the plausibility that Mark's gospel used the Elijah-Elisha narrative as a source.

EPISODIC STYLE

Mark's gospel is clearly a prose narrative; however, the narrative is not continuous but rather episodic. Collins describes this episodic nature well: "the work is composed of many blocks of independent material of different genres that are unified by being placed in a rough overall chronological framework."[16] These independent blocks are often connected by common themes, vocabulary, actions, or characters. While this episodic prose style is not foreign to Greco-Roman biography or historiography—

---

12. For these statistics, see Burridge, *What are Gospels*, 168–69.
13. Again, see Burridge for these statistics, *What are Gospels*, 139, 169.
14. Morgenthaler, *Statistik*, Table 3, 164.
15. This count is excluding 2 Kgs 8:16–29 and 13:1–13, material that is only loosely related to the narrative and that consists of a formulaic list of kings and their offspring.
16. Collins, *Mark*, 41.

Lucian's *Demonax* provides an example of the former genre and the works of Herodotus provide examples of the latter—it is rare, as both genres are predominantly characterized by a continuous prose style. It seems unlikely that in regard to narrative style Mark has patterned his gospel after either Greco-Roman biography or historiography, and it raises the question of what type of literature might the evangelist have patterned his gospel after. A possible answer to this question is not hard to find. The evangelist's sacred scriptures provided a perfect example. Much of the narrative of the Old Testament primary history (Genesis–2 Kings) shares the episodic style of Mark's gospel.[17]

Yet, an even more specific parallel to the episodic style of Mark's gospel is found in the Elijah-Elisha narrative. Two motifs link Mark's gospel more closely to the Elijah-Elisha narrative than other episodic OT historical narratives (e.g., those of Abraham, Jacob, Joseph, Moses, Joshua, Samuel, and David)—a miracle motif and a prophetic motif. In the span of nineteen chapters, Elijah and Elisha are the agents of a combined twenty-one miracles. They also make a combined eight prophecies about specific events that find their fulfillment in the narrative. No other OT narrative contains such a quantity and frequency of miraculous events and fulfilled prophecies. The only narrative that rivals the Elijah-Elisha narrative in its quantity of miraculous or prophetic events is that of Moses. But the narrative of Moses' life spreads these events over three long books (Exodus, Numbers, and Deuteronomy), making the frequency/intensity of miraculous events much lower in the Moses narrative than in the Elijah-Elisha narrative.[18] The quantity and frequency of miracle and prophetic episodes in the Elijah-Elisha narrative is closely paralleled by the quantity and frequency of similar episodes in Mark's gospel. In Mark, Jesus is the agent of twenty miracles, and he makes six prophecies that are specifically fulfilled within the narrative.[19] All of these episodes in Mark occur over a span of only sixteen chapters. There is no other literary work that provides a

17. See Aune, *Literary Environment*, 36–41.

18. That the deeds and life of Moses are at some level in the background of Mark's gospel seems plausible, but the OT narrative of Moses' life seems on the whole unlikely as a literary source for Mark.

19. These six do not include the prophecies made in chapter 13 because of the debate over whether these prophecies are *vaticinium ex eventu* or whether they refer to realities not yet experienced by the evangelist or his community. Clearly, prophecies regarding Jesus' parousia—found in chapters 13 and 14—had yet to find their fulfillment for the evangelist or his community, and they are not included in the count given here.

General Similarities between Mark and the Elijah-Elisha Narrative

better pattern for Mark's episodic style and content than the Elijah-Elisha narrative.

Therefore, again we see another close literary link between Mark's gospel and the Elijah-Elisha narrative. Both are characterized by an episodic style, with the episodes of both containing a high quantity and frequency of miracles and fulfilled prophecies.

GEOGRAPHICAL ORIENTATION/STRUCTURE

While the Markan evangelist begins the gospel with John the Baptist in the Judean wilderness near the Jordan, at the beginning of Jesus' ministry, he quickly moves it to Galilee (northern Israel). It is in Galilee and the north (including Tyre and Sidon) where the majority of Jesus' ministry will take place in Mark's gospel, (e.g., the majority of his healings [all but one], all of his exorcisms, his sea-related miracles, and his multiplication of loaves). It is not until chapter ten that Jesus and his disciples leave Galilee and the northern parts of Palestine and enter into Judah. After what is presumably a brief time in Judah, Jesus spends his final week in Jerusalem—a week that culminates in his death. The book ends with a promise that the resurrected Jesus will meet his disciples again in Galilee.

In Markan scholarship, much has been made of Mark's geographical orientation.[20] Some have argued that it reflects a conflict between the church in Jerusalem and the church in Galilee.[21] Others have argued that it serves Mark's concern for a Gentile mission and Gentile inclusion.[22] Some may still hold to the notion that this orientation actually represents the historical reality of Jesus' public ministry.[23] But virtually no scholar has suggested what seems to be a highly plausible explanation, namely that Mark's geographical orientation was borrowed from a literary source.

Again, the Elijah-Elisha narrative could provide just such a source for Mark's geographical orientation. After a brief introduction of Ahab

---

20. For example, see Lohmeyer, *Das Evangelium des Markus*, esp. 29; idem, *Galiläa und Jerusalem*; Lightfoot, *Locality and Doctrine*; Marxsen, *Mark the Evangelist*.

21. For example, see Kelber, *Kingdom in Mark*, and Weeden, *Traditions in Conflict*.

22. For example, see Theissen, *Gospels in Context*, 281–87.

23. Most interpreters however recognize that the historical Jesus likely went between Galilee and Jerusalem relatively frequently during his public ministry and that geographical orientation of the synoptic gospels is a later literary (or perhaps theological) construct rather than a historical one. See Moloney, "Fourth Gospel and the Jesus of History," 42–58 and Dunn, *Christianity in the Making*, 165–67.

and his surpassing wickedness, the Elijah-Elisha narrative begins with Elijah in the wilderness near the Jordan river, though it cannot be certain whether he is in Judah. The narrative then quickly moves to the north, to the region of Sidon. The large majority of the narrative then takes place in the northern kingdom of Israel. However, at the end of the narrative, it shifts to the south and focuses on the restoration of the temple in Jerusalem. It then briefly returns to the northern kingdom as it recounts the death of Elisha.

The parallels between the geographical orientation of both Mark and the Elijah-Elisha narrative are striking. While it is possible that these similarities are only coincidence and that Mark and the Elijah-Elisha narrative arrived at such similar geographical orientations independently, such an argument becomes more difficult to make in light of the other evidence that has already been put forth. Ultimately, this similarity is easily explained by Mark's use of the Elijah-Elisha material as a literary source/model.

CONCLUSION

None of the evidence we have presented here proves that Mark used the Elijah-Elisha narrative as a source. Yet, it is noteworthy that all of these similarities find an easy explanation in the theory that Mark is literarily dependent on the Elijah-Elisha narrative. Clearly this evidence increases the plausibility of such literary dependence, and is easily explained by it.

5

Mark 1:1–20 and the Elijah-Elisha Narrative

INTRODUCTION

We now begin our analysis of the Markan text in order to determine whether there is significant evidence of Markan literary dependence on the Elijah-Elisha narrative. Our analysis begins with the beginning of Mark's first chapter. As we noted in our evaluation of Dennis MacDonald's work, finding evidence of literary dependence in the early stages of a narrative is particularly significant, because ancient authors often left signals or clues to their readers regarding their literary sources at such stages.[1] Here we will look for any such signals and clues that might be embedded in the text. We will also look for clear examples of Markan imitation of the Elijah-Elisha narrative.

MARK'S OPENING CITATION

Mark's gospel is unique in that it opens with a quotation from Jewish scripture (1:2–3). This opening quotation combines Malachi 3:1 with Isaiah 40:3, even though the evangelist only cites the prophet Isaiah.[2] Here the evangelist gives the reader an obvious clue regarding the source mate-

---

1. See Sandnes, "*Imitatio Homeri*," 31–32.

2. While the wording of the citation in v. 2 is also quite similar to Exodus 23:20 ("Behold, I am sending my messenger before your face, so that he might guard you in the way"), the citation is likely of Malachi 3:1 ("Behold, I am sending out my messenger, and he will inspect the way before my face") for the following reasons: (1) In Mark's gospel, the opening prophecy is fulfilled by John the Baptist; (2) Malachi 3:1 refers to the eschatological figure of Elijah who is specifically referred to in Malachi 3:23–24; and (3) Mark clearly portrays John the Baptist as the eschatological figure of Elijah. For a discussion on this quote, see Collins, *Mark*, 135–36.

rial that has influenced and shaped his work, namely Jewish scriptures.[3] Many interpreters have used this quotation to claim that the text of Isaiah in particular has played a significant role in the formation and theology of the gospel.[4] But it is possible that Mark might also be pointing the reader to a particular figure in Jewish Scripture. Malachi 3:1 promises that God will send a messenger before he brings his judgment upon Israel. In Malachi 3:22 (LXX), it is quite clear that the messenger is the prophet Elijah: "And behold, I will send you Elijah the Tishbite before the great and glorious day of the Lord."[5] To the observant reader, Mark's opening citation alludes to the prophetic figure of Elijah. Such an allusion might very well function as a clue to the reader that the story of Elijah is an important background for the gospel. This allusion to Elijah alone means little, but it might become more significant if additional allusions to or clear imitation of the Elijah-Elisha narrative can be discerned.

JOHN THE BAPTIST AND ELIJAH

As we proceed through Mark's gospel, we quickly find additional allusions to Elijah in Mark's presentation of John the Baptist.[6] In fact, a strong case can be made that Mark's presentation of John the Baptist is an imitation of Elijah. Both Elijah and John the Baptist appear suddenly with virtually no introduction in their respective narratives. John's appearance in the wilderness and his baptismal work in the Jordan parallels Elijah's initial hiding in the wilderness near the Jordan. This parallel might even be seen as a reversal of sorts, as John is in the wilderness calling Israel to repent, and Elijah is hiding in the wilderness at a time when Israel is unwilling to repent. But perhaps the most convincing evidence that Mark's presentation of John is an imitation of Elijah is the description of the former's appearance. Mark's physical description of John the Baptist as one ἐνδεδυμένος τρίχας καμήλου καὶ ζώνην δερματίνην περὶ τὴν ὀσφὺν

---

3. See Sandnes, "*Imitatio Homeri*," 31–32.

4. Noteworthy examples include Marcus, *Way of the Lord*, 12–47; and Watts, *Isaiah's New Exodus*.

5. Author's translation.

6. Many interpreters have noted such allusions, but few have expressly claimed a Markan imitation of the Elijah-Elisha narrative in his presentation of John the Baptist. For other interpreters who recognize the similarities between the Markan John and Elijah, see Collins, *Mark*, 140–46; Marcus, *Mark 1–8*, 156–57; France, *Gospel of Mark*, 69; van Iersel, *Mark*, 96–97.

αὐτοῦ or "clothed with camel's hair, with a leather belt around his waist" (Mark1:6) also clearly recalls (imitates?) the appearance of Elijah (ἀνὴρ δασὺς καὶ ζώνην δερματίνην περιεζωσμένος τὴν ὀσφὺν αὐτοῦ or "a hairy man, with a leather belt around his waist" [2 Kgs 1:8]).

Here, the conclusion that Mark's presentation of John the Baptist is an intended imitation of Elijah in 1 and 2 Kings is strongly supported by the criterion of shared narrative details. Both men appear abruptly at the beginning of the narrative, are in the wilderness near the Jordan, are seeking the repentance of Israel, and are strikingly similar in appearance. The specific nature of the latter similarity—similarities marked by striking verbal agreement—makes the conclusion for imitation undeniable. That Mark later directly associates John the Baptist with Elijah (Mark 9:9–13) only confirms this conclusion.

MARK 1:12–20 AS AN IMITATION OF 1 KINGS 19:4–21

After Jesus' baptism by John, Mark contains three successive pericopes that resemble three successive pericopes in the Elijah-Elisha narrative.

1 Kings 19:4–21	Mark 1:12–20
Elijah in the Wilderness (4–14)	Jesus in the Wilderness (12–13)
God's Proclamation of Jehu as Israel's King who will restore God's Kingdom (15–18)	Jesus' Proclamation that the Kingdom of God is Near (14–15)
Elijah's Calling of Elisha (19–21)	Jesus' Calling of Disciples (16–20)

We have what appears to be a similarity in narrative structure/ordering of events. We will now examine each set of parallel pericopes to determine whether such a similarity in order does in fact exist and whether additional evidence might exist to support a case for literary imitation.

Parallel Wilderness Accounts

Many interpreters have noted similarities between the Markan account of Jesus' temptation in the wilderness, and Elijah's experience in the wilderness as recorded in 1 Kings 19:4–9. The obvious parallels include the time spent by each figure in the wilderness—forty days—and the care given by angels to both figures.[7] While these two details seem to

---

7. These details are noted by numerous commentators, including Gundy, *Mark*, 60–62; Marcus, *Mark 1–8*, 167–71; France, *Mark*, 83–87; Donahue and Harrington, *Mark*, 65–66; van Iersel, *Mark*, 101–4.

draw the two narratives together quite closely, some have rejected any intentional relationship between them. Hermann Mahnke rejects such a relationship based on what he believes to be significant differences: (1) Elijah is traveling, while Jesus is not; (2) Elijah is not tempted, while Jesus is; (3) Wild animals are not present with Elijah, but they are present with Jesus; and (4) the Elijah account does not mention forty nights, but only forty days.[8]

However, these arguments against Markan dependence on the Elijah-Elisha narrative are on the whole ignorant of the Greco-Roman practice of imitation, and are therefore unduly restrictive. As we have seen in our examination of Greco-Roman imitation, an author did not need to slavishly copy his source, but rather had the freedom to alter and adapt it to his/her narrative purposes. The examples we saw of this freedom in Virgil's use of Homer were numerous. Such authorial freedom easily explains the so-called "problematic" differences put forth by Mahnke. While Elijah is traveling through the wilderness to mount Horeb, such traveling does not fit Mark's narrative, so it is eliminated. Mark's deletion of "forty nights" from his rewriting could simply be the evangelist's desire to remove a redundancy from his source. Both of these noted differences are minor, and in light of the imitation practices of Greco-Roman authors, they do little to undermine a case for Markan imitation of the Elijah-Elisha narrative.

Yet, perhaps more significant is the claim that Elijah is not tempted during his time in the wilderness. But is such a claim accurate? We must consider what Elijah is actually doing in the wilderness. He is not there because God has called him there—as God's twice repeated question of "What are you doing here, Elijah?" would indicate—but rather he is there because Jezebel has threatened to take his life. He is in the desert because he is on the run. In fact, one could argue that he is on the run from his divine calling. A temptation seems very clear in the text, namely Elijah's temptation to abandon his divine prophetic call and to lie down and die (see 1 Kgs 19:4). We could argue that this struggle that Elijah clearly has over his divinely appointed role has then been abbreviated by the Markan evangelist and recast as Jesus' struggle with the temptations of Satan. In both stories, the prophetic figure overcomes their temptation.[9]

8. See Mahnke, *Die Versuchungsgeschichte*, 25–38.
9. Perhaps P. G. Walsh's description of Livy's imitative technique would be helpful here as it identifies a precedence for this Markan imitation: "Livy's literary approach can

Mark 1:1–20 and the Elijah-Elisha Narrative

The last objection offered by Mahnke, namely the lack of wild animals in the Elijah episode, can also be resolved. This detail, though absent in Elijah's wilderness experience as recorded in 1 Kings 19, is present in Elijah's wilderness experience as recorded in 1 Kings 17:4–7. In Elijah's first wilderness experience, he is in the presence of wild birds (crows/ravens) which bring him food to eat. Such wild birds could be the pattern for wild animals that are present in Mark 1:13. It is quite reasonable that in composing Jesus' wilderness temptation narrative, that the Markan evangelist conflated details from the two accounts of Elijah in the wilderness. As we saw in our examination of Virgilian imitation, such conflation was a common imitative technique.

Therefore, all the details of Jesus' wilderness temptation narrative, as recorded in Mark, find parallels in the wilderness experiences of Elijah. Both Elijah and Jesus are in the wilderness for forty days, both are tempted, both are attended to by angels, and both are in the presence of wild animals. The criterion of shared details strongly supports the conclusion that Mark's account of Jesus' temptation in the wilderness is imitating the Elijah-Elisha narrative.

Parallel Proclamations about the Kingdom of God

At first glance, one might find little similarity between Jesus' proclamation of the good news of the Kingdom of God in Mark 1:14–15 and God's proclamation to Elijah that he is to appoint Hazael as King of Aram and Jehu as King of Israel. The two proclamations neither share significant vocabulary and nor verbal agreement. But close examination of the Elijah-Elisha text shows that both proclamations share strong thematic similarities. God's proclamation is a response to Elijah's twice expressed frustration over Israel's idolatry and their rejection of Yahweh and his prophets. Through the actions of Jehu, Hazael, and Elisha, God is orchestrating the destruction of Israel's idolatrous leaders and a restoration of his centrality in the Kingdom of Israel. In essence, God is proclaiming that his kingdom is drawing near and the kingdom of Baal is about to fall.

---

thus be summarised as follows. He utilizes one main source, reorganizes the structural arrangement, and introduces new material to achieve more dramatic effects. He compresses or omits the less interesting content, using as criteria the purpose of his work and the interests of his audience. Then, in addition to these ... aims of *enargeia* [graphic presentation] and *syntomia* [compression], he seeks ... *saphēneia* [clarification] and *pithanotēs* [credibility in narration]." See Walsh, *Livy*, 190.

It is plausible that the Markan evangelist has recast—in a radical way—this proclamation in the Elijah-Elisha narrative as Jesus' proclamation about the coming Kingdom of God. Such a theory is strengthened by the fact that both proclamations of God's kingdom sit directly between a wilderness narrative and a "call" narrative.

Parallel Call Narratives

Many interpreters have argued that Mark's account of Jesus calling his first disciples is patterned after Elijah's calling of Elisha in 1 Kings 19:19–21.[10] Both stories begin with a master finding would-be disciples. In both stories, the would-be disciples are found working: Elisha is found plowing a field and Peter and Andrew are found fishing. The master in each respective story initiates the call of the would-be disciples. In both stories, the would-be disciples leave their livelihood in order to follow their new master. Each story ends with a response from the new disciples to their family. In addition to this similar ordering of events, the two stories also contain noteworthy verbal agreement that can be seen in the chart below.

1 Kings 19:19–21	Mark 1:16–20
Elijah finds Elisha (19)	Jesus finds the disciples (16, 19)
Elijah is found working (plowing) (19)	Disciples are found working (fishing) (16, 19)
Elijah initiates call (symbolic call) (19)	Jesus initiates call (verbal call) (17, 20)
Elisha leaves his livelihood (20)	Disciples leave their livelihood (18, 20)
Elisha's Response to Family (20–21)	Disciples' Response to Family (20)
Wording used to describe Elisha's response: ἀκολουθήσω ὀπίσω σου "I will follow after you" ἐπορεύθη ὀπίσω Ἠλιου "he went after Elijah"	Wording used to describe disciples response: ἠκολούθησαν αὐτῷ "They followed him" ἀπῆλθον ὀπίσω αὐτοῦ "they went after him"

There are certainly differences between the stories, but these differences can be explained by the differing narrative purposes of the author. They also reflect the common imitative practice of "intensification" that we

---

10. For examples, see Brodie, *Crucial Bridge*, 91; Collins, *Mark*, 156–57; Marcus, *Mark 1–8*, 183–84; van Iersel, *Mark*, 129–34.

Mark 1:1–20 and the Elijah-Elisha Narrative

often saw in Virgilian imitation.[11] For Mark, the number of disciples is intensified. Mark initially doubles the number of disciples from one (Elisha) to two (Peter and Andrew), with the latter being brothers. He then doubles the "calling" itself by repeating the call to two more disciples (James and John), another set of brothers. Therefore, through this progressive doubling, Mark intensifies the total number of disciples from one to four. Mark also intensifies the call in his narrative, moving from a symbolic call—the placing of a mantel on a disciple—to a strong verbal call—"Come after me, and I will make you fishers of human beings." The response of the disciples is also intensified. While Elisha is allowed to go back and say goodbye to his father and mother, Mark specifically states that James and John leave their father standing in the boat. This intensification is consistent with Mark's message of radical discipleship (for example, see Mark 8:34–38; 10:28–31).

Given the combined support of three significant criteria for establishing literary dependence—shared narrative details, shared narrative order, and verbal agreement—the case that Mark's account of Jesus' calling the first disciples is imitating Elijah's calling of Elisha is strong.

The Culmination of the Evidence

Here we have three successive pericopes in Mark's gospel that closely parallel three successive pericopes in the Elijah-Elisha narrative. Each set of pericopes follow the same general order: (1) wilderness temptation; (2) proclamation concerning the reign of God; and (3) calling of disciples. This evidence alone is a significant indicator of literary imitation; but in addition to this general similarity in order, each set of respective parallel pericopes contains striking similarities in narrative details, narrative order, theme, language, or some combination of these criteria. The chart below reflects this evidence clearly.

1 Kings 19:4–21	Mark 1:12–20
I. Elijah in the Wilderness (4–14)	I. Jesus in the Wilderness (12–13)
A. Forty Days and Nights in Wilderness (8)	A. Forty Days in Wilderness (13)
B. Attended to by Angels (5, 7)	B. Attended to by Angels (13)
C. Presence of Ravens (1 Kg 17:4–5)	C. Presence of Wild Animals (13)

---

11. Collins also notes Mark's intensification of the story (*Mark*, 157).

1 Kings 19:4–21	Mark 1:12–20
D. Tempted to Abandon Divine Calling (10, 14)	D. Tempted by Satan (13)
II. God's Proclamation of Jehu as Israel's King Who will Restore God's Kingdom (15–18)	II. Jesus' Proclamation that the Kingdom of God is Near (14–15)
III. Elijah's Calling of Elisha (19–21)	III. Jesus' Calling of Disciples (16–20)
A. Elijah finds Elisha (19)	A. Jesus finds the disciples (16, 19)
B. Elijah is found working (plowing) (19)	B. Disciples are found working (fishing) (16, 19)
C. Elijah initiates call (symbolic call) (19)	C. Jesus initiates call (verbal call) (17, 20)
D. Elisha leaves his livelihood (20)	D. Disciples leave their livelihood (18, 20)
E. Elisha's Response to Family (20–21)	E. Disciples' Response to Family (20)

These two blocks of texts clearly meet the criteria of shared narrative details, shared narrative order, and to a slight degree verbal agreement. The case for Markan literary dependence on the Elijah-Elisha narrative at this point is therefore quite strong.

CONCLUSION

Our analysis of Mark chapter one has provided significant evidence of Mark's dependence on the Elijah-Elisha narrative. Mark's opening quotation alludes to the prophet Elijah, possibly serving as a clue to the reader indicating the gospel's literary influences. Mark's presentation of John the Baptist is clearly imitating the figure of Elijah. Finally, we find that a large block of Markan text shows clear and obvious signs that it is dependent on the text of the Elijah-Elisha narrative.

6

Mark's Galilean Ministry and the Elijah-Elisha Narrative

INTRODUCTION

In this chapter we will analyze pericopes in Mark's account of Jesus' Galilean ministry (Mark 1:21—8:26) in order to discern any possible dependence on the Elijah-Elisha narrative. Four pericopes will be considered: (1) Jesus' healing of a leper (1:40–45); (2) Jesus' healing of a paralytic (2:1–12); (3) Jesus' and the Syrophoenician woman (7:24–30); and (4) Jesus' feeding of five thousand and four thousand (6:30–44; 8:1–10).

JESUS' HEALING OF A LEPER

In Mark's narration of Jesus healing a leper, we find a unique parallel to the story of Elisha healing Namaan, the leprous Syrian official (2 Kings 5:1–19).[1] While leprosy is not uncommon in biblical narratives/texts (Exod 4:6–7; Lev 13–14; Num 12:10–15; Deut 24:8; 2 Sam 3:29; 2 Kgs 5:20–27; 7:3–10; 15:5; 2 Chr 26:16–21; Matt 10:8//; Matt 11:5//), outside of Mark (and parallels), there are only two biblical accounts that narrate the healing of a leper—2 Kings 5:1–19 and Luke 17:11–19. Of these, only 2 Kings 5:1–19 provides us with a strong parallel to Mark's account. The fact that these two accounts are two of only three biblical narratives about the healing of lepers is in and of itself significant and suggests a possible literary relationship between them. When the parallels within the stories are considered, such a literary relationship becomes quite clear. In both stories, the leper initiates the healing (2 Kgs 5:5, 9; Mark 1:40). Both stories also make reference to "his hand" (τὴν χεῖρα αὐτοῦ) being placed on

---

1. This parallel is recognized by Brodie, *Crucial Bridge*, 91–92.

a leper (2 Kgs 5:11; Mark 1:41). In both stories, the leper is completely cleansed after the act of healing (2 Kgs 5:14; Mark 1:42). In fact, the language used in Mark and 2 Kings 5 to describe the healed state of both lepers is similar.

- 2 Kgs 5:14: ἐπέστρεψεν ἡ σὰρξ αὐτοῦ ὡς σὰρξ παιδαρίου μικροῦ καὶ ἐκαθαρίσθη ("His flesh was restored like the flesh of a young boy, **and he was [made] clean**")
- Mark 1:42: καὶ εὐθὺς ἀπῆλθεν ἀπ' αὐτοῦ ἡ λέπρα, καὶ ἐκαθαρίσθη ("Immediately the leprosy left him, **and he was made clean**)

In both descriptions, the first clause describes the new state of the healed men's skin, while the second clause uses the same word to declare that the men were made clean. Finally, both stories also contain a statement related to cultic ritual. 2 Kings 5 refers to Namaan's future worship in a temple, while Mark includes Jesus' instruction to the leper to make a sacrifice to the priest.

Not only do the two stories share these significant similarities in detail, but they also share a similar order.

2 Kings 5:1–18	Mark 1:40–45
Namaan seeks healing. (4)	Leper seeks healing. (40)
Elisha gives instructions for healing. (10)	Jesus touches the leper. (41)
Namaan is made clean by following Elisha's instructions. (14)	The leper is made clean by Jesus' touch. (42)
Namaan promises to only offer sacrifices to Yahweh. (17)	Jesus orders the healed leper to offer a sacrifice to the priest. (44)

Therefore, the criteria of shared narrative details and of shared narrative order support the conclusion that this Markan pericope is imitating the Elijah-Elisha narrative. Clearly the Markan evangelist has made changes to his source, but most of these Markan changes are explained by common imitative techniques. Mark has abbreviated the story significantly by omitting many of the details from the Elijah-Elisha account, (e.g., the leper's interaction with the kings, means of healing, the initial doubt of the leper, etc.). But as we have seen in Virgil's work, such abbreviation through omission was a common imitative practice. In some ways, these abbreviations even result in intensification. Mark has intensified the greatness of the miracle—and the miracle worker—by changing the means of the healing from bathing in a river to a healing touch and spoken word (note that Mark has transformed the means by which Namaan expected to be healed [1 Kgs 5:11] into the means by which Jesus actually heals the leper). The intermediary role of the miracle worker is minimized, making the miracle worker appear more powerful. For Mark, this change is consistent with Jesus' identity as God's messianic Son. Mark has also reversed the roles of some characters, changing Namaan's promise to offer sacrifices to Yahweh into Jesus' instruction to the leper to offer sacrifices to the priest. But again, such role reversals were quite common in Greco-Roman imitation.

When all the evidence is considered, the criteria of shared details and shared narrative order support the conclusion for literary dependence between these two accounts of a healed leper. The unique subject matter of these pericopes, namely the healing of a leper, also supports such a conclusion.

JESUS' HEALING OF THE PARALYTIC

Here we will consider the suggestion by Wolfgang Roth that Mark's account of Jesus healing a paralytic is modeled after the 2 Kings 1 account of King Ahaziah's fall from his roof. First, we should note that Mark's description of John the Baptist has already demonstrated his familiarity with 2 Kings 1—a description that we have noted imitates the description of Elijah found in this very passage. Mark's previous use of this Elijah-Elisha episode clearly establishes the plausibility that he might imitate it again at some point.

When we look at the stories closely, many notable similarities appear. Both have a man falling/be lowered from a roof. Both stories also have a man confined to a bed/mat—a reality that plays a prominent role in both stories. In 2 Kings 1, three times King Ahaziah's permanent confinement to his bed is mentioned (vv. 4, 6, 16), while in Mark's account of Jesus healing the paralytic, three references are made to the paralytic taking up his mat. Also in both stories, intermediaries are used between the divine representative and the injured person. In 2 Kings 1, Ahaziah sends messengers to the god Ekron, messengers who then meet Elijah and bring his message to the king. In Mark 2, the paralytic is brought to Jesus by four men. Yet despite these similarities, the stories are quite different. The Markan account is a story of faith and healing, while the Elijah-Elisha account is a story of apostasy and death. But might this significant difference—the opposite focus and outcome of both stories—actually be a positive sign for literary dependence? Roth suggests this very thing when he claims that the Markan account is an inversion (or a reversal) of the Elijah-Elisha account.[2] When we look at the two stories from this perspective, the previous similarities we noted take on additional significance. The chart below lays out the similarities between the narratives clearly.

2 Kings 1:1–17	Mark 2:1–12
A. King falls through the roof (2)	B. Man confined to bed—paralyzed (3)
B. King is confined to his bed (2, 4)	C. Man carried to Jesus by four people (3)
C. King sends messengers to pagan god (2)	A. Man is lowered through the roof (4)
D. Messengers meet Elijah (3)	D. Man meets Jesus (5)
E. Elijah recognizes lack of faith in Yahweh (3)	E. Jesus recognizes faith (5)
F. Elijah foretells of the king's impending death (4)	F. Jesus forgives and heals the man (5–12)

Regarding the details/structure of the story, the Markan evangelist has introduced some creative reversals. In the Elijah-Elisha episode, the King Ahaziah begins the narrative healthy. He then falls through a roof, an act that results in permanent confinement to his bed. In the Markan episode, the paralyzed man begins the narrative confined to his bed (mat). He then is lowered through a roof, an act that results in his healing. This reversal in details/structure, ultimately contributes to a Markan reversal of the story's theme. The pericope from 2 Kings recounts a movement from health to death by way of apostasy. But Mark's creative imitation has transformed the pericope, reversing it so that it recounts a movement from sickness to health by way of faith! Obviously, Mark has radically altered the original form of this imitated story, more so than we have seen in our previous examples. But such alterations are neither without explanation nor without precedence in the practice of Greco-Roman imitation. As we have seen in our analysis of Virgilian imitation, the reversal of narrative theme, structure, and outcome are quite common. Furthermore, the omission of

---

2. See Roth, *Hebrew Gospel*, 56.

narrative details and the addition of new details are also quite common imitative practices. The Markan evangelist has made this Elijah-Elisha narrative fit the gospel's narrative purposes and the alterations that we see reflect this fact.

While Mark's imitation of this Elijah-Elisha episode involves a reversal of narrative theme (Mark transforms an episode that moves from health to sickness by way of apostasy to an episode that moves from sickness to health by way of faith), central to both of these stories is a question regarding God's presence. In the Elijah-Elisha narrative, Ahaziah seeks a message from the pagan god of Ekron, Baal-zebub. It is this act of apostasy that leads Elijah to pose the question a question about God's presence in Israel: "Is it because there is no God in Israel that you are going to inquire of Baal-zebub, the god of Ekron?" (2 Kgs 1:3). In the Markan episode, the scribes question Jesus' ability to forgive sins: "Who can forgive sins but God alone?" (Mark 2:7). This question is ultimately a question about the presence of God in the ministry of Jesus, a question that will surface again later in Mark (see 3:19–30). We suggest this question about God's presence is at the heart of both stories, and that the outcome of the two stories reflect different responses to the question. In the Elijah-Elisha narrative, King Ahaziah ignores the presence of God in Israel; an act which results in his death. But in Mark's gospel, the paralytic—contra the scribes—acknowledges the presence of God in Jesus' ministry, an act which results in his healing. This central theme of God's presence also ties these two stories together.

The case for this Markan pericope's dependence on the Elijah-Elisha narrative is supported by the criteria of shared details and similarity in structure. It is also supported by the presence of a shared narrative theme. We grant that the similarities in detail and structure are perhaps not as straight forward as those seen in the previous pericopes we have examined. Clearly, the similarity of the stories on the macro level is less apparent. The similarity between some of the narrative details is less specific, and the similarity in narrative order/structure is less obvious. But despite their subtlety, these similarities are still clearly present, and we suggest are best explained by a literary relationship between these two narratives. Given the nature of ancient literary imitation, a conclusion for literary dependence between these stories is highly plausible, even if it is less certain than previous conclusions. Such a conclusion is certainly strengthened by the fact that more clear cases of Markan dependence on the Elijah-Elisha narrative have already been established. As we noted in our analysis of MacDonald, subtle evidence of imitation on its own is not convincing, but when it is combined with more clear evidence it becomes much stronger.

JESUS' MULTIPLICATION OF LOAVES

Mark's two narratives in which Jesus feeds thousands of people by multiplying loaves of bread (6:30–44 and 8:1–10) finds an obvious—and often recognized—parallel in the Elijah-Elisha narrative.[3] The shared details are numerous. All three stories take place in a context where food is needed. In each story, only a small amount of food is available, with each story specifying the amount. Both Elisha and Jesus give instructions that the small amount of food be distributed, and in all three stories, the instructions are met with doubt/hesitation.[4] In all three stories, the food is distributed to and eaten by a large number of people, with each story specifying the number of people present. Finally, at the end of each story, an abundance of food remains. These shared narrative details, as well as the shared order of events are laid out clearly in the chart below.[5]

Elisha (2 Kgs 4:42–44)	Jesus (6:30–44)	Jesus (8:1–10)
Hunger—famine in land (38)	Hunger—day w/out food (31)	Hunger—three days w/out food (1–2)
Small amount of food—twenty barley loaves + fig cakes (42)	Small amount of food—five loaves of bread + two fish (38)	Small amount of food—Seven loaves of bread + a few fish (5, 7)
Command to pass out food "Give to the men, so that they may eat" (42)	Command to provided food "Give them something to eat" (37)	Command to pass out food implied (2–3)

---

3. For other commentators who note the similarity between Jesus and Elisha multiplying loaves, see Marcus, *Mark*, 415–16; Moloney, *Mark*, 133; Donahue and Harrington, *Mark*, 209–11; van Iersel, *Mark*, 225–30.

4. Gundry argues that the disciples response to Jesus in vs. 37 is a real question, one that clarifies whether he actually wants them to go and purchase food for the large crowd; *Apology*, 324–25. However, many interpreters conclude that this question reflects doubt and incredulity at the request. See Marcus, *Mark*, 407, 418; France, *Mark*, 266; Hooker, *Mark*, 166; Lane, *Mark*, 228; Pesch, *Das Markusevangelium*, 1:351.

5. These similarities are laid out in a similar way by Marcus, *Mark*, 415–16, and Donahue and Harrington, *Mark*, 209.

Mark's Galilean Ministry and the Elijah-Elisha Narrative

Elisha (2 Kgs 4:42–44)	Jesus (6:30–44)	Jesus (8:1–10)
Servant responds with doubt/hesitation (43)	Disciples respond with doubt/hesitation (37)	Disciples respond with doubt/hesitation (4)
Command is repeated (43)	Command to the disciples to sit the people down (39)	Command to the crowd to sit down (6)
Food distributed by a servant (44)	Food distributed by disciples (41)	Food distributed by disciples (6)
A large number of people eat (100) (44)	A Large number of people eat (5,000) (42)	A Large number of people eat (4,000) (8)
Extra food remains (44)	Extra food remains (12 baskets full) (43)	Extra food remains (7 baskets full) (8)

That the Markan pericopes are dependent on the Elijah-Elisha narrative is strongly supported by the criteria of shared narrative details and shared narrative order. To deny such dependence seems impossible. Certainly there are differences between the two stories, but these differences are easily explained, and do not stretch the bounds of Greco-Roman imitation. Mark has clearly expanded what is a brief episode in the Elijah-Elisha narrative, adding and changing a number of narrative details. Some of these changes can be attributed to Markan intensification of the Elijah-Elisha account—an intensification that reflects that Jesus is greater than Elisha. Jesus uses a smaller amount of food than Elisha, and feeds a larger amount of people. While the Elijah-Elisha narrative indicates that food was left over, the Markan narrative specifies the amount that is left over—twelve and seven baskets full—perhaps emphasizing the greatness of the miracle. Perhaps this intensification is best expressed through Mark's doubling of the miracle itself, indicating the significance it plays in his gospel. Other changes to the narratives such as the setting of the story—an isolated location—and the breaking and blessing of the food can be explained by narrative or theological motivations, i.e., the setting fits Mark's portrayal of Jesus' teaching outside of cities and populated areas, and the breaking and blessing of the bread might reflect the Eucharistic practices of the early church.[6] Mark has taken a relatively simple miracle episode from the Elijah-Elisha narrative, and given it a prominent and significant place in the gospel. Not only is this Markan pericope saturated

---

6. See Quesnell, *Mind of Mark*; cf. Marcus, *Mark 1–8*, 509–11; Ernst, *Das Evangelium nach Markus*, 226.

with narrative and theological significance, but it is essentially repeated in the gospel, reinforcing its significance for the reader.

It seems impossible to deny that the Markan evangelist has used the 2 Kings account of Elisha multiplying bread as a pattern for his double account of Jesus doing the same thing.[7] That the Elijah-Elisha narrative is a literary source for Mark at this point in the gospel is virtually certain.

THE SYROPHOENICIAN WOMAN

Few interpreters have compared Mark's pericope of the Syrophoenician woman (7:24–30) with the account of Elijah and the widow of Zarephath (1 Kings 17:7–16).[8] But we would like to identity some interesting similarities that may point to the former pericope as a creative imitation of the latter. The stories share a handful of similar narrative details. It is noteworthy that both stories take place in Syria, north of Israel. The Elijah-Elisha episode takes place in Sidon, while the Markan episode takes place in Tyre. While the cities are different, they are regularly linked in biblical texts. Mark's reference to Tyre would quickly bring the twin Syrian city Sidon to the reader's mind as well. Both stories also involve a gentile woman and her child/children in distress. This is a noteworthy similarity, because there are only three accounts in the entire biblical witness of prophetic figures bringing aid to a Gentile woman and her child/children—two of these three are the stories we are considering here, and the third also occurs in the Elijah-Elisha narrative. Based on these unique similarities, a perceptive Markan reader would quickly associate this pericope with the Elijah-Elisha narrative.

Another interesting similarity between the Markan episode of the Syrophoenician woman and Elijah-Elisha episode of the widow at Zarephath is that both stories are the first part of a two-part miracle-narrative block. The episode of Elijah and the widow at Zarephath is divided into two different miracle stories. 1 Kings 17:7–16 recounts Elijah meeting the widow and providing her with food. This story is followed by

---

7. We must be clear that in claiming that Mark's doubled account of Jesus feeding multitudes is literarily dependent on the Elijah-Elisha narrative, we are not excluding the influence of other sacred Jewish texts on these pericopes. Clearly the pericope has also been influenced by the book of Exodus and the stories of Moses providing manna in the wilderness (Ex 16). But here we suggest that the primary literary model for this story is 2 Kgs 4:42–44.

8. Roth has suggested a possible relationship, but few interpreters have considered his case. See Roth, *Hebrew Gospel*, 51–52.

Mark's Galilean Ministry and the Elijah-Elisha Narrative

an account of Elijah healing the widow's son (1 Kings 17:17–24). These two stories are clearly a distinct literary unit. The Markan account of the Syrophoenician woman is also immediately followed by another miracle story, Jesus' healing of deaf and mute man (Mark 7:31–37). These stories also appear to form a single literary unit, one tied together by the narrative thread of Jesus' travels. The first story (the Syrophoenician woman) begins by describing Jesus' journey into Gentile territory, a literary marker that separates the episode from the one immediately preceding it. The second story (the healing of the deaf and mute man) begins with a continued description of Jesus' travels, travels that continue from the region of Tyre, into Sidon, and then to the region of the Decapolis.[9] The description of Jesus' travel narrative ends with this second pericope, ending the narrative unit. That both of the narratives in question are the first part of two-part literary unit, only further ties them together.

The relationship between these two pericopes become even more intriguing when we look more closely at the dialogues between the women and the respective prophetic figures. We first notice that the respective dialogues share the same structure: (1) character "A" makes an initial request for help; (2) character "B" refuses help; (3) character "A" rebuts the reason for refusal; and (4) character "B" grants the initial request. While this similarity in structure is intriguing, it alone is not overwhelming evidence for literary dependence. However, when we compare the specific details of the corresponding parts of these dialogues, the case for dependence becomes much stronger.

---

9. Though it is unrelated to our present interests, we should note that here the Markan evangelist seems to be geographically confused. Interpreters have made much of his description of Jesus' journey. See Cranfield, *Gospel According to St. Mark*, 250; Nineham, *Gospel of St. Mark*, 40, 203; Lührmann, *Das Markusevangelium*, 132; Theissen, *Gospels in Context*, 242–45.

Mark and the Elijah-Elisha Narrative

Elijah and the Widow at Zarephath (1 Kgs 17:8–16)	Jesus and the Syrophoenician Woman (Mark 7:24–30)
Character "A": Request for help (10–11)	Character "A": Request for help (26)
καὶ ἐβόησεν ὀπίσω αὐτῆς Ηλιου καὶ εἶπεν αὐτῇ λαβὲ δή μοι ὀλίγον ὕδωρ εἰς ἄγγος καὶ πίομαι 11 καὶ ἐπορεύθη λαβεῖν καὶ ἐβόησεν ὀπίσω αὐτῆς Ηλιου καὶ εἶπεν λήμψῃ δή μοι ψωμὸν ἄρτου ἐν τῇ χειρί σου	καὶ ἠρώτα αὐτὸν ἵνα τὸ δαιμόνιον ἐκβάλῃ ἐκ τῆς θυγατρὸς αὐτῆς
And Elijah called after her and said to her, "Now bring to me a little water in a vessel, and I will drink." And she went and he called to her and said, "Now bring to me a morsel of bread in your hand."	She asked him to cast the demon out of her daughter.
Character "B": Refusal to Help (12)	Character "B": Refusal to Help (27)
καὶ εἶπεν ἡ γυνή ζῇ κύριος ὁ θεός σου εἰ ἔστιν μοι ἐγκρυφίας ἀλλ᾽ ἢ ὅσον δρὰξ ἀλεύρου ἐν τῇ ὑδρίᾳ καὶ ὀλίγον ἔλαιον ἐν τῷ καψάκῃ καὶ ἰδοὺ ἐγὼ συλλέγω δύο ξυλάρια καὶ εἰσελεύσομαι καὶ ποιήσω αὐτὸ ἐμαυτῇ καὶ τοῖς τέκνοις μου καὶ φαγόμεθα καὶ ἀποθανούμεθα	καὶ ἔλεγεν αὐτῇ· ἄφες πρῶτον χορτασθῆναι τὰ τέκνα, οὐ γάρ ἐστιν καλὸν λαβεῖν τὸν ἄρτον τῶν τέκνων καὶ τοῖς κυναρίοις βαλεῖν
And the woman said, "As surely as the Lord your God lives, I do not have a loaf (of bread), but only a handful of flour in a water jar, and a small amount of olive oil in a flask. And behold, I am collecting two small pieces of wood, and I will go, and I will prepare it for myself and my children, and we will eat it and die."	And he said to her, "let the children be fed first, for it is not good to take the bread of the children and throw it to the dogs"

Mark's Galilean Ministry and the Elijah-Elisha Narrative

Elijah and the Widow at Zarephath (1 Kgs 17:8–16)	Jesus and the Syrophoenician Woman (Mark 7:24–30)
Character "A": Rebuttal of Refusal Reasons (13)	Character "A": Rebuttal of Refusal Reasons (28)
καὶ εἶπεν πρὸς αὐτὴν Ηλιου θάρσει εἴσελθε καὶ ποίησον κατὰ τὸ ῥῆμά σου ἀλλὰ ποίησον ἐμοὶ ἐκεῖθεν ἐγκρυφίαν μικρὸν ἐν πρώτοις καὶ ἐξοίσεις μοι σαυτῇ δὲ καὶ τοῖς τέκνοις σου ποιήσεις ἐπ' ἐσχάτου	δὲ ἀπεκρίθη καὶ λέγει αὐτῷ· κύριε· καὶ τὰ κυνάρια ὑποκάτω τῆς τραπέζης ἐσθίουσιν ἀπὸ τῶν ψιχίων τῶν παιδίων
And Elijah said to here, "Take courage. Go and do what you have spoken; but first make a small loaf of (bread) and bring it to me, and then lastly you will make one for yourself and your children."	But she answered and said to him, "Lord, even the dogs under the table eat the crumbs from the children's table."
Character "B": Request Granted (15)	Character "B": Request Granted (29)
καὶ ἐπορεύθη ἡ γυνὴ καὶ ἐποίησεν καὶ ἤσθιεν αὐτὴ καὶ αὐτὸς καὶ τὰ τέκνα αὐτῆς	καὶ εἶπεν αὐτῇ· διὰ τοῦτον τὸν λόγον ὕπαγε, ἐξελήλυθεν ἐκ τῆς θυγατρός σου τὸ δαιμόνιον
And the woman went and did what Elijah told her; and he, she, and here children ate.	Then he said to her, "For this word, go— the demon has left your daughter."

The initial request for aid and the final granting of the request in both episodes have no direct notable similarities in details. However, we do find striking similarities in the initial refusal to help and in the rebuttal of the reason for refusal.

While the initial refusals to grant a request are quite different, they have one striking similarity. Both explanations of refusal are grounded in the same notion, namely the need for children to eat bread first. The woman tells Elijah that she cannot offer him any bread, because the little material that exists for making bread must be used to feed herself and her children. In Jesus' response to the Syrophoenician woman, he uses a metaphor that references the need for children to eat bread first. Throughout the entire Old and New Testament, this motif of children eating bread first is only found in these two stories (not including parallels). Therefore, the presence of this unique detail in the same section of two structurally identical dialogues is significant and closely ties these pericopes together.

As we see in the chart above, this similarity is strengthened by shared vocabulary.

Again, we find another unique similarity when we look at the two rebuttals. Both contain the notion of people eating spare or left over food. Elijah's tells that woman that she and her children can eat the food that remains after he has eaten, while the Syrophoenician woman continues Jesus' metaphor by claiming that even dogs are allowed to eat the crumbs that fall from the children's table, i.e., the food that is left over. Again, shared vocabulary also strengthens the similarity. That both of these parallel rebuttals share this same motif is striking and hardly seems coincidental.

Here we argue that Mark's pericope of Jesus and the Syrophoenician woman has creatively imitated the account of Elijah and the widow at Zarephath (1 Kgs 17:8–16). For the most part, Mark has maintained the primary characters in the story, though he has not identified the woman as a widow, and he has replaced the widow's children with a specific child—a daughter. He has also changed the central need in the story, changing the widow's need for food into the woman's need for her daughter's exorcism. These imitative changes are fairly straightforward and easy to discern. However, to discern Mark's imitation of the dialogue between Elijah and the widow requires careful attention. As we have already demonstrated, Mark has kept the structure of the dialogue in the Elijah-Elisha episode. But while keeping the structure of the dialogue, he has transformed it in many significant ways. Perhaps most noticeably, he has reversed the roles of the dialogue participants. In the account of Elijah and the widow, it is Elijah who presents the request, and the widow who refuses it. However, in Mark, it is the woman who makes the request, and Jesus who refuses it. Another obvious change is Mark's transformation of the initial double request from Elijah (the request for water and the request for bread) into a single request from the woman (the request for an exorcism for her daughter). But Mark's next imitative transformation is less obvious. Mark has transformed the refusal of the widow, a refusal that claims there is only enough bread to feed the widow and her children, into the refusal of Jesus, a refusal that claims the children must be fed bread first. Mark then transforms Elijah's rebuttal, a rebuttal that instructs that the prophet be fed first and then the widow and her children, into the rebuttal of the woman, a rebuttal that acknowledges that even dogs (referring to the woman and child) receive left over food that falls to the floor. Finally, Mark imitates the widow's willingness to grant Elijah's request, with Jesus' willingness to grant the Syrophoenician widow's request. The granting of both requests results in blessing for the women of these stories—the widow of Zarephath receives food to sustain her children, while the Syrophoenican woman receives the health and wellbeing of her daughter. This imitation is laid out clearly in the following chart.

1 Kings 17:7–16	Mark 7:24–30
Elijah in Sidon (8)	Jesus in Tyre (24)
Elijah meets a Gentile widow and her children who are starving (10)	Jesus meets a Gentile woman who has a sick daughter (25)
Four part dialogue between Elijah and the widow (10–15)	For part dialogue between Jesus and the woman (26–29)
1. Request: Elijah asks the widow for water and bread (10–11)	1. Request: The woman asks Jesus to heal here daughter
2. Refusal: The widow claims there is only enough food for herself and her children (12)	2. Refusal: Jesus' uses a metaphor—"Let the children be fed first" (27)
3. Rebuttal: Elijah instructs the woman to feed him first and then her and her children can eat what is left over.	3. Rebuttal: The woman continues the metaphor—"Even the dogs eat the crumbs [what is left over!] that fall from the children's table" (28)
4. Request Granted: The widow provides food for Elijah and her faith results in abundant food for herself and her children (15)	4. Request Granted: Because of the woman's faith, Jesus casts the demon from her daughter (29)

But perhaps more compelling than the explanation for "how" Mark's gospel has imitated this Elijah-Elisha episode, is the explanation for "why" the Markan evangelist has done so. The primary purpose of the Markan pericope is not to recount an exorcism, though exorcisms seem to play an important role in Mark's gospel. Rather the purpose of the Markan pericope is to establish precedence for Gentile inclusion.[10] A handful of stories from the Elijah-Elisha narrative establish precedence for such inclusion—one of which is Elijah's ministry to the widow of Zarephath.[11] This story therefore provides a perfect model for Mark to use in order

---

10. See Moloney, *Mark*, 144–48; Hooker, *Mark*, 184; Corley, *Private Woman, Public Meals*, 95–102; Marcus, *Mark 1–8*, 465–71; et al.

11. The Lukan evangelist clearly recognizes such a precedence being established in this Elijah episode—see Luke 4:25–26.

to address the issue of Gentile inclusion. When we look closely at the Markan episode, we see that Mark's creative imitation of the Elijah-Elisha episode's dialogue plays on the very realities of Gentile inclusion present in that episode. Jesus' claim that the children (Jews) should be fed first and their food not given to dogs (Gentiles), recalls Elijah's instructions regarding who should eat first, though the language reflects that of the widow desiring that her children eat first. The rebuttal of the Syrophoenician woman recalls the reality that even though Elijah ate first, there were still "crumbs" left over for the Gentile widow and her children. In a sense, the Markan Jesus' tests the woman's knowledge of God's care for Gentiles, and the woman passes the test by recalling God's previous faithfulness to a woman in distress.

When the cumulative evidence is considered there is a strong case for literary dependence between Mark's account of the Syrophoenician woman and the 1 Kings account of Elijah and the widow of Zarephath. Both the criteria for shared narrative details and the criteria for shared narrative structure/order of events support the conclusion for literary dependence. Furthermore, the theme of Gentile inclusion present in both stories serves as strong corroborating evidence for literary dependence. It strains credulity to suggest that two stories that share as much in common as these stories do have no literary relationship. The case for dependence between these particular stories is made even stronger when we consider the previous examples of dependence that we have established between Mark's gospel and the Elijah-Elisha narrative.

CONCLUSION

We have provided four significant examples of Markan dependence on the Elijah-Elisha narrative. Two of these examples are clear and straight forward examples of Mark imitating the Elijah-Elisha narrative—namely Jesus' healing of a leper and the multiplication of the loaves. The additional two examples (Jesus' healing of the paralytic and encounter with the Syrophoenician woman) are, on the surface, more obscure and reflect more creative Markan imitative techniques. However, all four examples are supported by our established criteria, and ultimately, they strengthen the case for Mark's use of the Elijah-Elisha narrative as a source. Additionally noteworthy is the fact that we see significant variety Mark's imitative methods, variety we also saw in Virgil. We see that Mark is not restricted any one particular paradigm of imitation, but exercises a good deal of freedom and creativity in his imitative technique.

7

Mark's Passion Predictions and the Elijah-Elisha Narrative

INTRODUCTION

VIRTUALLY ALL MODERN MARKAN interpreters consider Peter's confession at Caesarea Philippi and the passion predictions that follow it to be a watershed moment in Mark's gospel.[1] Because of the significance this section of Mark's narrative holds, any textual signals or clues to Markan source material would likewise be significant. Here we will examine Mark 8:27—10:45, in which we find Peter's confession at Caesarea Philippi and Jesus' three passion predictions. Again we will look for textual clues that might point Mark's reader to the author's sources, as well as for examples of direct Markan imitation of feature/episodes from the Elijah-Elisha narrative.

EXPLICIT TEXTUAL SIGNALS: ELIJAH IN PETER'S CONFESSION AND THE TRANSFIGURATION

When we come to this middle section of Mark's gospel, it does not take long to find explicit references to Elijah. In fact, within the span of twenty-four verses, Mark uses Elijah's name six times. At Peter's confession at Caesarea Philippi, he notes that some of the people identify Jesus as Elijah (8:28). In the transfiguration narrative, Elijah is physically present with Jesus and Moses, and his name is mentioned twice (9:4–5). Immediately following the transfiguration narrative, Jesus and his disciples discuss the eschatological significance of Elijah, and mention his name three times

---

1. For examples of such conclusions, see Moloney, *Mark*, 171–73; Collins, *Mark*, 397; France, *Mark*, 326; van Iersel, *Mark*, 270–77; Hooker, *Mark*, 200–203; Pesch, *Markusevangelium*, 27–46; J. Marcus, *Mark 8–16*, 602–15; Boring, *Mark*, 234–48.

(9:11–13). In this span of text, Elijah's name occurs more times than Jesus' name, with Elijah occurring six times and Jesus occurring only five. Clearly, the Markan evangelist is drawing the reader's attention to the character of Elijah and quite plausibly to the Elijah-Elisha narrative as well. Though it is not certain, these references to Elijah could very well be textual clues by which the Markan evangelist is pointing the reader to one of his primary sources. Such a conclusion is strengthened by the previous examples we have seen of the evangelist imitating the Elijah-Elisha narrative, and it would be made stronger if such imitation could be identified in this central section of Mark's gospel.

THE PASSION PREDICTIONS

Many Markan interpreters have concluded that the Markan passion predictions, in their present form and number (3x), are to some extent creations of the evangelist who has introduced them into his life of Jesus for literary and/or theological reasons.[2] However, few interpreters have been able to offer an explanation for why the Markan evangelist has presented the passion predictions in this manner? Why is the prediction given three times? Or why are the predictions offered at different geographical locations, as Jesus moves from Caesarea Philippi in the north to Jerusalem in the south? No interpreter has provided a possible pattern or source for the evangelist's three-fold repetition of Jesus' passion predictions. But much has been made of the literary function of these predictions in Mark's gospel. Yarbro-Collins, among others, has noted that each passion prediction

---

2. Some interpreters believe that any notion of Jesus' prediction of his death is simply a creation of the early church, thus the Markan passion predictions are created *ex nihilo*, e.g., Bultmann, *Synoptic Tradition*, 152; idem, *Theology of the New Testament*, 1.29; Käsemann, "Problem of the Historical Jesus," 37; Perrin "Towards an Interpretation," 10–21. Other interpreters believe that behind the Markan passion predictions is a historically reliable tradition; see for example, Francis Moloney who suggests that the second passion prediction might actually be quite close to the actual words of the historical Jesus; Moloney, "The End of the Son of Man?" 280–90; idem, *Mark*, 171, esp. n. 2. Raymond Brown reaches similar conclusions in *The Death of the Messiah*, 2:1468–91. Yet, regardless of whether these predictions are seen as Markan creations or partially grounded in historical reminiscences, virtually all scholars will agree that the way they appear in Mark's gospel, e.g., repeated three times, increasing in specificity with each successive prediction, etc., are either literary or theological constructs, e.g., see Branscomb, *Gospel of Mark*, 153; Nineham, *Mark*, 229; Dibelius, *Tradition to Gospel*, 225–26; Hooker, *Mark*, 204–5; Evans, *Mark*, 9–12. For further discussion, see Evans, "Did Jesus Predict His Death," 82–97.

is a part of a larger literary pattern.³ First, the evangelist provides a prediction of death (and in two instances resurrection; see 8:31 and 10:32–34). Second, the evangelist notes in varying ways the failure of Jesus' disciples to comprehend the prediction. Third, the evangelist concludes with a particular teaching of Jesus on discipleship. She also notes that Mark has placed as bookends to these successive passion narratives accounts of Jesus healing a blind person. The passion narratives, therefore, function to teach on blindness as it relates to discipleship. But Yarbro-Collins, like other interpreters who read Mark's passion predictions in a similar way, gives no possible literary pattern or precedent that Mark might be working from. Is this pattern that Yarbro-Collins and other have identified simply created by the Markan evangelist, or could it be an example of creative imitation?

Here we suggest that this literary pattern finds a striking precedent in the Elijah-Elisha narrative. In 2 Kings 2, we find three successive predictions made to Elisha regarding Elijah's ascension. In v. 3, the sons of the prophets in Bethel ask Elisha, εἰ ἔγνως ὅτι κύριος σήμερον λαμβάνει τὸν κύριόν σου ἐπάνωθεν τῆς κεφαλῆς σου or "Do you know that today the Lord will take your Lord from above your head?" This question is repeated (the second prediction) in v. 5 by the sons of the prophets in Jericho. The third prediction comes in v. 9 but breaks the previous pattern and comes from Elijah himself when he tells Elisha, αἴτησαι τί ποιήσω σοι πρὶν ἢ ἀναλημφθῆναί με ἀπὸ σοῦ or "Elisha, ask what I might do for you before I am taken from you." Therefore, in the Elijah-Elisha narrative, we find three successive predictions to Elisha regarding Elijah's ascension.

But what are more striking than these three successive predictions of Elijah's final departure are the patterns that these predictions follow. After each of the first two predictions of Elijah's departure, we find a response from Elisha. In each response, Elisha explains that he understands that his master will be taken from him: "Yes, I know. Be quiet." Then, after Elisha's response to each of the first two predictions of Elijah's departure—responses that reflect his understanding—the narrative immediately moves to scenes in which Elisha refuses to leave his master. In these scenes, Elijah asks Elisha to stay behind as Elijah travels on to a new city, but Elisha swears an oath that he will not leave his master (2 Kgs 2:4, 6). Therefore, both the first two passion predictions in Mark and the

---

3. Collins, *Mark*, 397; Perrin, "Towards an Interpretation," 7–8; Moloney, *Mark*, 172.

predictions regarding Elijah's ascension in 2 Kings 2 follow a strikingly similar pattern: (1) both begin with a prediction of final departure (death/ascension); (2) both follow this prediction with a statement regarding the disciples' understanding of the prediction—confusion vs. understanding; and (3) both follow this prediction-response pattern with teachings or actions related to faithful discipleship.

Up to this point we have only examined the first two departure predictions of both Mark's gospel and the Elijah-Elisha narrative. We now turn our attention to the third respective predictions of both texts. Collins claims that the third Markan passion prediction follows that of the first two: (1) prediction; (2) confused response; and (3) teaching on discipleship. But here we suggest that Collins is only right if the last two elements of the pattern are combined in the third Markan passion prediction. For the third passion predictions is not followed by an immediate statement regarding the disciples' understanding of it, as are the first two. Instead, it is followed by a story in which James and John request seats of honor when Jesus comes into his glory. Certainly this story implies the disciples' confusion regarding Jesus' immediately preceding passion prediction, but the narrative never makes an explicit connection between James and John's request and such confusion. This story therefore seems to function differently than the confused responses of the disciples that are explicitly linked to the two preceding passion predictions.

This clarification regarding Collin's literary analysis is important because it lays the ground work for further comparisons between the Markan passion predictions and the predictions of Elijah's departure in 2 Kings 2. The third departure predictions in both Mark and 2 Kings break from the pattern established by the first two departure predictions in these narratives. What is striking is that they both break from their previous patterns in surprisingly similar ways. Both of these third departure predictions are followed by requests from a disciple or disciples. James and John ask for places of power when Jesus comes into his glory. Elisha asks for a double portion of Elijah's spirit (presumably the Spirit of God) after he has departed. Both responses to these requests describe the difficulty in fulfilling them. Jesus' tells his disciples, "You do not know what you are asking" (Mark 10:38), and Elijah explicitly states, "You have asked something difficult of me" (1 Kgs 2:10). Finally, the responses to both requests are deferred to God, as those of whom the request is made are unable in and of themselves to grant it. Jesus tells James and John, "to sit at my right hand or at my left is not mine to grant, but it is for those for whom it has been prepared" (Mark 10:40). Elijah tells Elisha, "If you see me while I am being taken up, it will be as you requested and if you do not see me, it will not be" (2 Kgs 2:10).

An additional element that links Mark's passion predictions with the predictions of Elijah's departure in 2 Kings 2 is that both sets of predictions are set within the narration of a journey. The predictions of Elijah's departure take place as Elijah and Elisha are traveling from Gilgal to the Jordan, the place of Elijah's departure. Along the way, they stop at Bethel and Jericho, before they reach the Jordan. It is at each of these destinations that we receive a prediction of Elijah's departure. Mark 8:27—10:45, the section in which we find the Markan passion predictions, is also the narration of a journey. The journey begins in Caesarea Philippi and ends in Jerusalem, the place of Jesus' crucifixion. Along the way, the text notes that Jesus and his disciples pass through Galilee, Judea and beyond the Jordan, and finally head toward Jerusalem. Like the predictions of Elijah's departure, the passion predictions are distributed between these geographical locations. In fact, before each passion narrative, a new geographical location is provided by the author.

The similarities we have described above are laid out clearly here.

Predictions of Elijah's Departure	Predictions of Jesus' Passion
1st Prediction: (2 Kgs 2:3–4)	1st Prediction: (Mark 8:31–38)
In Bethel (3)	In Caesarea Philippi (27)
a. Prediction of final departure (3)	a. Prediction of death (31)
b. Statement indicating a disciple's understanding of the prediction (3)	b. Statement indicating disciples' failure to understand the prediction (32)
c. Example of a faithful disciple (4)	c. Teaching on discipleship (34–38)
2nd Prediction: (2 Kgs 2:5–6)	2nd Prediction: (Mark 9:30–10:31)
In Jericho (5)	In Galilee (30–37)
a. Prediction of final departure (5)	a. Prediction of death (9:31)
b. Statement indicating a disciple's understanding of the prediction (5)	b. Statement indicating disciples' failure to understand the prediction (9:32)
c. Example of a faithful disciple (6)	c. Teaching on discipleship (9:33–37)

Mark's Passion Predictions and the Elijah-Elisha Narrative

Predictions of Elijah's Departure	Predictions of Jesus' Passion
3rd Prediction: (2 Kgs 2:9–11)	3rd Prediction: (Mark 10:32–40)
Crossing the Jordan to place of ascension (9)	On the way to Jerusalem—the place of crucifixion (32)
a. Prediction of final departure (9)	a. Prediction of final departure (33–34)
b. A disciple's request for power (9)	b. Disciples' request for power (35–37)
c. The request is identified as difficult (10)	c. The request is identified as difficult (38–39)
d. The request can only be fulfilled by God (10)	d. The request can only be fulfilled by God (39–40)

The case that Mark's central section is dependent on the Elijah-Elisha narrative in 2 Kings 2 is quite strong. It is supported by the criterion of shared narrative details/themes, including three predictions of departure and death, the final journey of prophetic figures, the theme of faithful discipleship, and a request for power from a disciple/disciples. But the case is made largely on the strength of the criterion of similar narrative structure/order. Both narratives present the three prediction of death/departure at successive geographical destinations within the context of a prophet's final journey. Each successive prediction follows a strikingly similar pattern; with the third prediction in both narratives breaking with the pattern of the previous two and following a distinct pattern its own. What is most impressive is the complex nature of this shared structure. That two narratives could independently produce such similar narrative structures is highly improbable, and therefore, literary dependence is an unavoidable conclusion.

Clearly the Markan evangelist's imitation here is both clever and creative. The three predictions from the Elijah-Elisha narrative have been diffused/dispersed in Mark's central section, occupying its beginning, middle, and end, and he has surrounded it with additional narrative material—much of it relating to the theme of discipleship. Yet, as we saw in Virgilian imitation, such diffusion was a common technique. Mark's gospel has also clearly reversed a number of significant details. It has turned the predictions made by others about the prophetic figure into predictions made by the prophetic figure himself—a reversal that certainly enhances the power of the prophetic figure.[4] It has also turned statements regarding Elisha's understanding of his master's departure into statements regarding the disciples' failure to understand Jesus' suffering and death. Mark has also expanded elements from the Elijah-Elisha episode. The predictions themselves have been transformed, reflecting changes in detail and structure—changes demanded by Mark's narrative, and perhaps by historical traditions. Elishah's example of faithful discipleship has been replaced by direct teachings regarding discipleship. The source of these teachings is unknown, but their placement here in Mark's narrative is discernibly patterned after the faithfulness of Elisha.

Markan Diffusion/Dispersal of 2 Kings 2:1-11:

2 Kings 2:1-11	Mark 8:27—10:45
	Confession at Caesarea Philippi (8:27-30)
	1st Passion Prediction (8:31—9:1)
	Prediction (8:31)
	Confusion/Peter's rebuke (8:32)
	Teaching on discipleship (8:33—9:1)
1st Prediction of Departure (3-4)	Transfiguration (9:2-8)
Prediction (3)	Discussing the Role of Elijah (9:9-13)
Statement of understanding (3)	Healing the a Boy with an Evil Spirit
Example of faithful discipleship (4)	(9:14-29)
2nd Prediction of Departure (5-6)	2nd Passion Prediction (9:30-37)
Prediction (5)	Prediction (30-31)
Statement of understanding (5)	Confusion over prediction (32)
Example of faithful discipleship (6)	Teaching on discipleship (33-37)
3rd Prediction of Departure (9-10)	Another Exorcist (9:38-41)
Prediction (9)	Teaching on Temptation (9:42-50)
Request for power (9)	Teaching about Divorce (10:1-12)
Request is difficult (10)	Jesus Blesses Children (10:13-16)
Only God can grant the request (10)	The Rich Man (10:17-31)

---

4. For a discussion on the possible significance of Jesus predicting his own death, see Winn, *Purpose of Mark's Gospel*, 119-21.

Mark's Passion Predictions and the Elijah-Elisha Narrative

2 Kings 2:1-11	Mark 8:27—10:45
	3rd Passion Prediction (10:32-40)
	Prediction (32-34)
	Request for Power (35-37)
	Request is difficult (38-39)
	Only God can Grant the Request (39-40)
	Teaching on Discipleship (10:41-45)

CONCLUSION

Elijah's final journey with his disciple Elisha and the predictions of Elijah's departure found in 2 Kings 2, provide the Markan evangelist with the perfect model both for Jesus' final journey to Jerusalem and for introducing Jesus' death. The evangelist creatively uses the structure of this Elijah-Elisha episode as the basic structure for his entire central section. As demonstrated above, this literary dependence between 2 Kgs 2:1-11 and Mark's central section is strongly supported by the criteria of shared narrative details and shared narrative structure/order. Markan imitative methods are easily discerned and understood, and they are consistent with techniques that were common in Greco-Roman imitation. Additionally, this imitation is signaled to the reader by the frequency of Elijah's name during the first twenty-four verses of the Mark's central section. Therefore, the case for Mark's dependence on the Elijah-Elisha narrative of 1 and 2 Kings continues to grow stronger as our analysis of the Markan text continues.

8

The Parable of the Wicked Tenants and the Elijah-Elisha Narrative

INTRODUCTION

MARK'S PARABLE OF THE wicked tenants (12:1–12) has received a great deal of attention from Markan interpreters. A significant amount of this attention has focused on the influence of Jewish Scriptures on the parable's meaning and formation. Virtually all scholars recognize that the "vineyard song" of Isaiah 5:1–7 plays a crucial role in understanding both the parable and its formation.[1] Attention is also given to Psalm 118, which is quoted directly by the Markan evangelist at the conclusion of the parable.[2] However, no Markan interpreters have considered the parable's possible relationship to the Elijah-Elisha narrative. Here, we argue that in addition to the "vineyard song" of Isaiah 5, 2 Kings 9 played a significant role in the formation of the parable of the wicked tenants.

---

1. For discussion on Isaiah's influence on Mark's parable of the wicked tenants, see Aus, *Wicked Tenants*; Evans, "Vineyard Parables," 82–86; idem, *Mark*, 210–40; Weren, "The Use of Isaiah 5,1–7," 1–26; Jeremias, *Parables of Jesus*, 70–73; Collins, *Mark*, 538–49; Moloney, *Mark*, 232–33; France, *Mark*, 456; Marcus, *Mark 8–16*, 810–11; Boring, *Mark*, 328–29. For discussion of the way in which the vineyard song may have been understood by first century Jews, readers should consult 4Q500; see Baumgarten, "4Q500," 1–6; Brooke, "Use of Scripture," 268–94.

2. For example, see Black, "Old Testament in the New Testament," 1–14; Brooke, "4Q500," 288. For those who see the quotation of Psalms 118 as inauthentic and attribute it to either the Markan evangelist or the early church see Carlston, *Triple Tradition*, 178–90; Lohmeyer, "Das Gleichnis," 242–59; Klostermann, *Das Markusevangelium*, 120–21; Schmid, *Gospel according to Mark*, 217–18; Gnilka, *Das Evangelium nach Markus*, 142; Pesch, *Markusevangelium*, 2:213; Hooker, *Mark*, 276–77; Moloney, *Mark*, 232 n. 87.

The Parable of the Wicked Tenants and the Elijah-Elisha Narrative

ISAIAH 5 AND THE PARABLE OF THE WICKED TENANTS

Before we consider a possible relationship between the parable of the wicked tenants and the Elijah-Elisha narrative, we will first consider the relationship between Isaiah 5 and the parable, noting the elements of the parable that it does and does not account for. In Isaiah 5:1–7 (LXX), "the vineyard song," God describes the kingdom of Israel as a vineyard that he has planted and cared for.[3] Despite the care and nurture that God has shown his "beloved" vineyard, it has produced thorn bushes (ἀκάνθας, LXX) rather than grapes. Because of the vineyard's failure to produce fruit, God will destroy it. The vineyard song is therefore a declaration of God's judgment upon Israel for its failure to produce the fruit of righteous living.

As many interpreters have noted, there are striking similarities between Isaiah's "vineyard song" and Mark's parable of the wicked tenants. Both passages open with descriptions of a vineyard. In Isaiah, God says, "I placed a fence around it (the vineyard)," while in Mark, the owner of the vineyard "put a fence around it." Also, in Isaiah, God says, "and I dug out a vat in it," while in Mark, the owner of the vineyard "dug a vat for the wine press." Lastly, in Isaiah, God says "and I built a tower in the middle of it," while in Mark the owner of the vineyard "built a watch tower" in it. The direct verbal similarities are seen clearly in the chart below.

Isaiah 5:2	Mark 12:1
καὶ **φραγμὸν περιέθηκα** καὶ ἐχαράκωσα καὶ **ἐφύτευσα ἄμπελον** σωρηχ καὶ **ᾠκοδόμησα πύργον** ἐν μέσῳ αὐτοῦ καὶ **προλήνιον ὤρυξα** ἐν αὐτῷ	**ἀμπελῶνα** ἄνθρωπος **ἐφύτευσεν** καὶ **περιέθηκεν φραγμὸν** καὶ **ὤρυξεν ὑπολήνιον** καὶ **ᾠκοδόμησεν πύργον**
"And **I placed a fence around it** and I fortified it; and I planted a choice vine; and **I built a tower in it**; and **I dug a vat in it**."	"And a certain man planted a vineyard; and **he placed a fence around it**; and **he dug a vat**; and **he built a tower**."

---

3. As we have been doing throughout this project, we are looking primarily at Mark's use of the Septuagint. Most interpreters conclude that Mark's parable of the wicked tenants is directly dependent on the Septuagintal version of the "vineyard song." For example, see Collins, *Mark*, 545; Marcus, *Mark 8–16*, 802, 811; Mell, *Die "anderen" Winzer*, 97–117. Craig Evans, though he acknowledges dependence on the Septuagint, also sees the influence of the Hebrew text on the parable as well. See Evans, *Mark*, 224–228.

From these similarities, it is clear that the Markan evangelist is drawing his description of the vineyard from Isaiah's "vineyard" song. This fact has led interpreters to rightly conclude that the vineyard in Mark's allegorical parable represents the people of Israel. Beyond these similarities few others remain, though it should be noted that both of these passages carry the theme of God's judgement. Therefore, Isaiah 5 leaves many features of Mark's parable unaccounted for. While it accounts for the vineyard, and the vineyard owner, it does not account for the other characters of the parable (tenants, messengers, and a son) or the actions of sending and rejecting messengers. Clearly some might claim that no source is needed to account for these additional features, and that they are merely the creation of an early Christian community, the Markan evangelist, or Jesus himself. Such a claim is possible, but since Mark has already demonstrated a strong dependence on Jewish scripture for certain features of this parable, that the other features of the parable might likewise find a similar literary source seems highly plausible. Given Mark's use of the Elijah-Elisha narrative at previous points in the gospel, it is prudent to consider this same narrative in order to find source material for the parable of the wicked tenants.

SUMMARIZING 2 KINGS 9

Two Kings 9 begins with Elisha sending one of his disciples to anoint Jehu as the new King of Israel. Jehu's anointing is the result of God's judgment on the house of Ahab, and it is Jehu whom God has chosen to destroy the house of Ahab and restore Yahweh worship in Israel. After Jehu is anointed king, he conspires against Jehoram, the son of Ahab and current King of Israel. Jehu goes to Jezreel in order to overthrow and kill Jehoram who is recovering from battle wounds. As Jehu approaches Jezreel, he is seen by a watchman, and Jehoram sends a messenger to meet Jehu. When the messenger meets Jehu and asks if he comes in peace, Jehu replies "What do you have to do with peace? Follow behind me." The watchman sees the messenger fall in behind Jehu, and tells the king that the messenger is not returning. The king then sends a second messenger, but achieves the same result. Finally, Jehoram himself goes to meet Jehu, and asks if he comes in peace. Jehu tells the king there will be no peace until Jezebel is killed, and he subsequently kills Jehoram. This meeting takes place in the property (a vineyard) that was once owned by Naboth but stolen from him by King

The Parable of the Wicked Tenants and the Elijah-Elisha Narrative

Ahab. Jehoram's death on this property fulfils God's promised judgment on Ahab for killing Naboth and stealing his vineyard.

EXPLAINING THE ALLEGORY IN THE PARABLE OF THE WICKED TENANTS

Before we begin to draw comparisons between 2 Kings 9 and Mark's parable of the wicked tenants, it is important that we first explain the significant allegorical features of the parable. The planter/owner of the vineyard clearly represents God. As we noted above, the vineyard itself represents the Jews or the people of Israel, or as some have suggested the temple.[4] The wicked tenants clearly represent Israel's leaders, or more specifically the temple authorities (see 11:27 and 12:12). The messengers represent God's prophets, and the son clearly represents Jesus, who according to Mark is God's messianic son (see Mark 1:1, 1:11, and 9:7).[5] The allegory

---

4. The vast majority of interpreters equate the vineyard in Mark's gospel with Israel, or more specifically, the people of Israel. See Evans, *Mark*, 232; Collins, *Mark*, 545; Brooke, "4Q500," 268–94 (Brooke more specifically sees the vineyard as Jerusalem, though it represents Israel—"Israel in miniature." Collins concurs with Brooke's conclusion.); Marcus, *Mark 8–16*, 811; Boring, *Mark*, 328; van Iersel, *Mark*, 364–65; Donahue and Harrington, *Mark*, 337. E. Lohmeyer argues that the vineyard represents the temple itself, and not the people/nation of Israel in general; see Lohmeyer, "Das Gleichnis," 242–59; idem, *Lord of the Temple*, 44. However, few interpreters have been convinced by Lohmeyer. The fact that Isaiah 5 explicitly links the vineyard with Israel in v. 7, and that the symbol of a vineyard is frequently used in the Hebrew scriptures to represent Israel (e.g., Isa 27:2–6; Jer 2:21; 12:10; Ps 80:8; etc.) strongly suggests that Mark is equating the vineyard with Israel in this parable. Also working against the conclusion that the vineyard represents the temple are the common allegorical readings of Isaiah 5:1–7 in Second Temple Judaism. 4Q500 and 1 Enoch 89:56, 66b–67 among other Second Temple texts identify the tower of Isaiah 5:2 as the temple, and the vat as the temple's altar. Since readers in the Second Temple period understood these specific details as symbols of the temple, it seems unlikely that the Markan evangelist would include these same details yet still intend the reader to equate the vineyard with the temple also. See Gundry, *Apology*, 684, for an argument against interpreting the vineyard of Mark 12 as the temple. Offering an altogether different understanding of the vineyard symbolism in Mark is Francis Moloney, who argues that the vineyard should be more specifically identified with the Kingdom of God. See Moloney, *Mark*, 232.

5. A handful of interpreters have argued that the son in the parable of the wicked tenants is best identified with John the Baptist; see Stern, *Parables in Midrash*, 193–95; Mann, *Mark*, 462–63. However, the majority of interpreters reject this conclusion. For a sound refutation of this position, Evans is useful: (1) no single tradition exists in which John is identified as the "son" whereas that identification is frequently used of Jesus, particularly in Mark's gospel; (2) the parable is a response to a question regarding Jesus' authority, not John's; (3) John the Baptist is executed by Herod Antipas, while the temple authorities

therefore relates the antagonistic relationship that has long existed between God and the rulers of his people. Like the vineyard in the story, God entrusted his people to the care of tenants, Israel's kings and priests. But when God desired to guide these leaders by sending them prophets, the leaders rejected them. Finally, God sought to guide his people through his messianic son Jesus, but like the prophets before him, the son is rejected and killed. The consequence of these leaders' actions will be the loss of their power, as God will take his people away from them and entrust their care to others.

COMPARING 2 KINGS 9 AND THE PARABLE OF THE WICKED TENANTS

Now that we have explained the features of Mark's allegory in the parable of the wicked tenants, we can begin comparing the parable with the account of Jehu's rebellion in 2 Kings 9. The two stories share a number of narrative details and narrative themes. Both stories involve the sending of messengers who fail to accomplish their given task; both involve the corrupt leadership of Israel—the wicked tenants and the house of Ahab; in both stories a vineyard plays an important role; and both describe the demise and replacement of Israel's corrupt leadership.

We will elaborate on these similarities in order to better establish their significance. As we noted, both of these stories involve the sending of multiple messengers who fail in there mission. In the account of Jehu's rebellion, Jehoram sends multiple messengers to Jehu, as Jehu is approaching the city of Jezreel in his chariot. But these messengers join Jehu, and fail to bring news back to their master. In the parable of the wicked tenants, the owner of the vineyard sends messengers to his tenants requesting his share of the vineyard's produce, but after being beaten and insulted (some even killed!), these messengers fail to bring anything back to their master. Another similarity regarding messengers is that the final messenger in both stories, a person of great importance, is killed. In 2 Kings 9, the final messenger is the King of Israel himself who is killed by Jehu, while in the parable of the wicked tenants the messenger is the son of the vineyard owner who is killed by the tenants. The similarities are

---

orchestrate Jesus' execution in Mark; see Evans, *Mark*, 230. For other interpreters who reach similar conclusions, see Lührmann, *Markusevangelium*, 199; Lagrange, *Saint Marc*, 283; Moloney, *Mark*, 233; Donahue and Harrington, *Mark*, 338; France, *Mark*, 460–61.

noteworthy: (1) both stories include the sending of multiple messengers; (2) in both stories the messengers fail in their mission; (3) in both stories the final messenger is someone of great significance; (4) and in both stories the final messenger is killed.

Another similarity is the centrality of Israel's corrupt leadership in both stories. In the parable of the wicked tenants, the tenants have turned against their master, the owner of the vineyard, and as noted above they have abused and killed not only his messengers but also his son. In the story of Jehu's rebellion against Jehoram, Jehoram is the son of the late King Ahab and the Queen Jezebel. The sins of Ahab and Jezebel are many, including the outright disobedience of Yahweh's instructions (1 Kgs 20:39–43), the worship of Baal and Asherah (1 Kgs 16:31–34), and the murder and persecution of Yahweh's prophets (1 Kgs 18:3–5; 19:1–3). But the sin for which God promises the utter destruction of Ahab and his house is Ahab and Jezebel's murder of Naboth and their confiscation of his vineyard (1 Kgs 21).

The sin of Ahab and Jezebel of killing Naboth and stealing his vineyard leads to the next similarity between the parable of the wicked tenants and Jehu's rebellion. The parable of the wicked tenants uses a vineyard as a symbol for Israel, a symbol that is certainly borrowed from the vineyard song of Isaiah 5. However, in the story of Jehu's rebellion, a vineyard is also significant, though not explicitly mentioned. As noted above, it is Ahab's confiscation of Naboth's vineyard that leads to the destruction of his family. Jehu is God's agent to bring about this destruction. And while the account of Jehu's rebellion does not specifically mention a vineyard, it does specifically mention "the property of Naboth" that was confiscated by and still held by Ahab's family. It is in this property, which the reader clearly knows is a vineyard (1 Kings 21), that Jehu places the dead body of Jehoram and specifically recounts the murder of Naboth and the wrongful confiscation of his property. Therefore, in the account of Jehu's rebellion, Ahab's illegitimate possession of a vineyard is the direct cause of the destruction of his royal house. In the parable of the wicked tenants, it is the attempt to wrongfully gain possession of a vineyard that leads to the tenants' destruction.

Finally, in both stories, the corrupt leadership of Israel is removed and new leadership is instituted. In Mark's gospel, the leadership of the people of Israel will be (or has been) taken away from the temple authorities and handed over to others (possibly the Romans). In the Elijah-Elisha narrative, the stewardship/leadership of the nation of Israel has been taken away from the family of Ahab and handed over to Jehu.

In addition to these shared narrative details and themes, the two stories have significant similarities in structure. The two stories begin with the rightful owner seeking to claim what belongs to him. Jehu is seeking to take his God given role of Israel's king from the corrupt king Jehoram. The vineyard owner is seeking to claim the share of his vineyard's produce from the corrupt tenants. Both stories then describe a series of messengers being sent, but in both stories the messengers fail their master in their task. Both stories send a final messenger, a figure of great importance. This final messenger is killed in both stories. Finally, both stories conclude with the destruction of corrupt leaders and the establishment of new leadership. In 2 Kings 9, Jehu becomes the new king of Israel, while in the parable of the wicked tenants; the vineyard is entrusted to new tenants.

An additional structural similarity is that both of these stories occur in close narrative proximity to a story that involves the cleansing of a temple. The parable of the wicked tenants comes shortly after Jesus' cleansing of the temple and the subsequent withering of the fig tree (likely a symbol of the temple's destruction). The account of Jehu's execution of King Jehoram comes shortly before Jehu's destruction of Baal's prophets in the temple of Baal—essentially cleansing Israel of idolatry.

The following chart lays out the similarities in both structure and detail.

Jehu's Rebellion (2 Kings 9:14–26)	The Parable of the Wicked Tenants (Mark 12:1–12)
	Story preceded by a cleansing of Israel's temple (Mark 11:15–25)
Jehu, God's anointed king comes to take kingship from the corrupt king, Jehoram (14–16)	The vineyard owner seeks his share of the vineyard's produce from corrupt tenants (2)
Corrupt king sends a messenger to the anointed king—messenger fails (17–18)	Vineyard owner sends a messenger to corrupt tenants—messenger fails (2–3)
Corrupt king sends a messenger to the anointed king—messenger fails (19–20)	Vineyard owner sends a messenger to corrupt tenants—messenger fails (4)
	Vineyard owner sends a messenger to corrupt tenants—messenger fails (5)

The Parable of the Wicked Tenants and the Elijah-Elisha Narrative

Jehu's Rebellion (2 Kings 9:14–26)	The Parable of the Wicked Tenants (Mark 12:1–12)
Corrupt king himself goes to the anointed king (20–21)	Vineyard owner sends his own son to the corrupt tenants (6)
Corrupt king is killed by the anointed king (22–24)	Son is killed by corrupt tenants (7–8)
By removing the corrupt king, the anointed kings (the new ruler of Israel) rights the wrong of a stolen vineyard. (25–26)	Because of the death of his son, the vineyard owner destroys the corrupt tenants and places new leaders in charge of the vineyard. (9)
Story followed by cleansing Israel of Baal's temple/prophets (10:18–25)	

THE CASE FOR IMITATION

The evidence that Mark's parable of the wicked tenants is literarily dependent on Jehu's rebellion in 2 Kings 9 is significant. The two episodes share a number of significant details and themes, including the centrality of corrupt leaders; the sending of multiple messengers (all of whom fail); the sending of a significant figure who is killed, the presence of a vineyard, and the ultimate defeat of corrupt leaders. But more than simply sharing these details and themes, the two stories order or structure these shared details and themes in a strikingly similar way. That two stories would independently share such similar details and structure seems highly improbable, making the conclusion for literary dependence quite strong.

Clearly the stories have significant differences, and the Markan evangelist's imitation has been quite creative. Again the evangelist has introduced some significant reversals, the most significant of which we find in the sending of the messengers. In the episode of Jehu's rebellion, it is the corrupt king Jehoram who is sending the messengers to the rightful king, while in the parable of the wicked tenants, it is the owner of the vineyard sending messengers to corrupt tenants. This reversal also forces Mark to transform the final messenger from a corrupt significant figure (Jehoram) into an innocent significant figure (the vineyard owner's son). Other characters in the account of Jehu's rebellion have also been changed by the evangelist out of necessity. In both the 2 Kings 9 episode of Jehu's rebellion and Mark's parable of the wicked tenants, the protagonist is God. In 2 Kings 9, this protagonist is represented by the newly anointed king,

Jehu, while in Mark, the protagonist is represented by the vineyard owner. Both stories also share the same antagonist, namely the corrupt leaders of Israel. But while in 2 Kings 9, this antagonist is represented by the corrupt king Jehoram, in Mark the antagonist is represented by corrupt tenants of a vineyard.

We suggest that the Markan evangelist has created this parable by bringing together two texts from Jewish Scripture; the "vineyard song" of Isaiah 5:1–7, and the account of Jehu's rebellion found in 2 Kings 9. The source of the vineyard motif clearly comes from Isaiah's vineyard song, and like Isaiah, Mark used the image of a vineyard to represent the people of Israel. But Mark then turns to a narrative in Jewish Scripture to provide the narrative details of the parable. The Elijah-Elisha narrative provides a highly attractive place to which the Markan evangelist could turn. Central to the narrative are perhaps Israel's most corrupt leaders, Ahab and Jezebel, who wrongfully confiscate a vineyard. Corrupt leaders and a vineyard are both central to Isaiah 5:1–7! The account of Jehu's rebellion, in which God enacts judgment upon Israel's corrupt leaders and vindicates the murderous theft of a vineyard, becomes a suitable narrative model for the construction of the parable of the wicked tenants. The parable as a whole is then linked to the messianic text of Psalm 118.

CONCLUSION

The Elijah-Elisha narrative, in which the corruptions of Israel's leaders takes center stage, provides the Markan evangelist with the perfect narrative model for constructing a parable through which Jesus addresses similarly corrupt leaders. The evangelist brings together the vineyard motif of Isaiah 5 and God's judgment of Israel's corrupt leaders in 2 Kings 9, to form the parable of the wicked tenants. While most Markan interpreters have already recognized the parable's use of Isaiah 5, none have recognized the parable's relationship to Jehu's rebellion in 2 Kings 9. Yet, here we have provided significant evidence that strongly demonstrates a literary relationship between these two texts. Markan imitation of 2 Kings 9 is supported by the criteria of both shared narrative details/themes and shared narrative structure. The imitative techniques that we see the evangelist use here are consistent with Greco-Roman imitative practices. Therefore, as we continue to move through the Markan text we see another example of Mark's dependence on the Elijah-Elisha narrative.

9

Mark's Passion and Resurrection Narratives and the Elijah-Elisha Narrative

INTRODUCTION

IT IS LIKELY SAFE to say that Mark's Passion and Resurrection narratives have received more scholarly attention than any other part of the gospel. As Martin Kahler has famously claimed, Mark's gospel is a "passion narrative with an extended introduction."[1] It is to these well-studied Markan narratives that we now turn to determine whether they bear any signs of a literary relationship with the Elijah-Elisha narrative. We will again look for textual clues that might signal to the reader the author's source material, as well as for clear examples of direct imitation.

EXPLICIT TEXTUAL CLUES: MARK'S PASSION AND RESURRECTION NARRATIVES

When we come to the end of Mark's gospel, we find far fewer explicit textual clues directing the reader to the Elijah-Elisha narrative than we found at the beginning (Mark 1, see chapter five above) or middle of the gospel (Mark 8:27—10:45, see chapter seven above). Elijah is directly mentioned only two times during Mark's crucifixion narrative—after the people mistakenly understand Jesus' cry "Eloi, Eloi," as a cry to Elijah for deliverance (see Mark 15:34–36). But other than these two occurrences, no direct reference or obvious allusion/echo of Elijah or Elisha is discernible. However, closer analysis of the two narratives demonstrates more continuity than these initial textual clues might indicate.

---

1. Kahler, *Historical Jesus and the Historic*, 80n11. It must be noted that I disagree with Kahler's assessment of Mark's gospel.

PETER'S TRIPLE DENIAL OF JESUS AND THE ELIJAH-ELISHA NARRATIVE

The historicity of Peter's denial of Jesus is largely accepted by New Testament interpreters, though many feel the various accounts of the denial found in the canonical gospels have been largely influenced by the early church and/or the evangelists themselves.[2] One of the features that many interpreters have argued is not historical but rather was a creation of either the early church or the Markan evangelist is the triple occurrence of the denial. But if a triple denial is not historical, the obvious question is where did it come from? Many interpreters suggest that through one redactional effort or another by the Markan evangelist the tradition was transformed from a single denial to a triple denial.[3] However, given the notorious difficulty in both detecting Markan redactional activity and also identifying hypothetical sources in Mark's text, these types of solutions remain at best speculative.[4] Surprisingly, no interpreter has been able to offer an extant literary source that could have provided the Markan evangelist with a model for a triple denial. This is even more surprising when such a model can be found in the Jewish Scriptures that the evangelist clearly knows well and has incorporated into the gospel.

As we have already seen, in the account of Elijah's final journey with his disciple Elisha (2 Kings 2), Elijah asks Elisha three times to stay behind while he goes on ahead to a new destination. However, each time, Elisha refuses to leave his master and swears an oath to such an effect. This episode from the Elijah-Elisha narrative offers significant similarities to Peter's triple denial of Jesus—similarities that make it a highly plausible source for Mark's account of the triple denial. Both stories involve a pow-

---

2. For examples of interpreters who conclude that Peter's denial of Jesus was a historical event, see Brown, *Death of the Messiah*, 615; Meier, *A Marginal Jew*, 242–44; Dunn, *Jesus Remembered*, 774; Sanders, *Historical Figure*, 164; Evans, *Mark*, 463. Brown lists a number of older interpreters who come to the same conclusion, including J. Weiss, Dibelius, Taylor, Lietzmann, E. Meyer, Schniewind, and Dinkler; see Brown, *Death*, 615. A handful of notable interpreters have rejected the historicity of this event, including R. Bultmann, M. Goguel, and most noteworthy G. Klein. See Klein, "Die Verleugnung," 285–328.

3. For examples of scholars who make such conclusions, see Masson, "Le reniement de Pierre," 24–35; Dewey, "Peter's Curse," 96–114 (it should be noted that Dewey feels the question of this tradition's historicity is unanswerable).

4. On the significant difficulties that vex attempts to identify Markan redaction, see Black, "Markan Redactor," 19–39; idem, *Disciples according to Mark*.

erful prophet and his prominent disciple. Elisha is the successor of Elijah, and one whom Elijah has specifically called to follow him. In Mark, Peter is the pre-eminent disciple and the representative for Jesus' successors. He also was specifically called by Jesus to follow him. Both stories are set in the context of the prophet's final departure or death—Elijah is about to ascend into heaven, and Jesus is about to be crucified. Both stories specifically address a disciple's willingness to remain faithful to the master. In both stories, the disciple's willingness to remain faithful is evidenced through a response to a direct statement or question from another individual. In both stories, the opportunity to demonstrate faithfulness by responding to the direct statement or question is repeated three successive times. Finally, while there is no exact verbal agreement between Peter's denials and Elisha's faithful response, there is some similarity between the language of Elisha and Peter's earlier promise to Jesus that he would never abandon him.

1. Elisha's faithful response (2 Kings 2:2, 4, 6): ζῇ κύριος καὶ ζῇ ἡ ψυχή σου εἰ καταλείψω σε (as the Lord lives and your soul lives, I will not leave you)

2. Peter's promise of faithfulness (Mark 14:31): ἀν δέῃ με συναποθανεῖν σοι, οὐ μή σε ἀπαρνήσομαι (even if it is necessary for me to die with you, I will not deny you)

In the first clause of both of these statements, we find a contrast between death and life: "as your soul lives" compared to "even if it is necessary for me to die with you." The second clauses are quite similar, with the primary difference being demanded by the narrative, i.e., the verb change from "leave" to "deny."

In light of our criteria for literary dependence, the case that Mark's account of Peter's triple denial of Jesus is modeled after Elisha's triple affirmation of Elijah is quite strong. We have demonstrated significant similarities in narrative detail and theme, and there exists a general similarity in the ordering of these details as well. There are even some small similarities in language that might further tie these two stories together. Additionally, as we saw in chapter seven, the evangelist has already used this episode of the Elijah-Elisha narrative, and in particular he has used this expression of Elijah's faithfulness as a pattern for his teaching on faithful discipleship. Therefore, we should not be surprised to see the evangelist return to this very episode to again address the issue of faithful discipleship (or unfaithful discipleship!).

Clearly, the Markan evangelist has used the technique of reversal here, transforming Elijah's triple affirmation of faithfulness into Peter's triple denial. We have seen that such reversals were not only common in Greco-Roman imitation, but also quite common in the Markan evangelist's own imitative practice. Virtually every example we have considered to this point of Markan imitation has evidenced the technique of reversal.

As we have demonstrated, there are significant reasons to conclude that Mark's account of Peter's triple denial of Jesus is an imitation of Elisha's triple affirmation of Elijah. If this case is accepted, then not only do we have further evidence that the Elijah-Elisha narrative was a significant literary source for Mark's gospel, but we also have a plausible explanation for how a general tradition of a Petrine denial of Jesus was multiplied into a triple denial.

THE CENTRALITY OF RELIGIOUS CORRUPTION IN TEMPLE WORSHIP

Though the closing chapters of the Elijah-Elisha narrative (2 Kings 9–12) and Mark's gospel (11:15—15:39) are quite different, they do share one distinct central theme. At the end of both narratives, temples, in particular their corruption and cleansing, play a central role. In the Elijah-Elisha narrative, the closing chapters describe the demise of Israel's and Judah's corrupt leadership and the eradication of Baal worship from both nations. This process begins with the anointing and ascension of Jehu as King of Israel, an event we discussed in the previous chapter. It is Jehu who kills Israel's King Jehoram, the son of Ahab, along with Jezebel and the rest of Ahab's family. Jehu also kills Ahaziah the King of Judah, an event that will set in motion restored leadership and restored temple worship in the southern nation. After removing Ahab's family, Jehu turns his attention to eradicating Baal worship from Israel. Under the false pretense of a grand celebration of Baal, Jehu calls all the prophets and followers of Baal to the god's temple and subsequently has them killed. He then destroys the temple of Baal itself, turning it into a latrine.

The narrative then shifts from a focus on Israel, to a focus on Judah and Jerusalem. After the death of Ahaziah, his young son Jehoash becomes the king. Under the guidance of the priest Jehoiada, the new king has the

Mark's Passion and Resurrection Narratives

temple of Baal destroyed, along with its priest. The new king also restores Yahweh worship among the people of Judah, and he begins a restoration of the temple in Jerusalem that had fallen into disrepair.

As many interpreters have noted, the temple plays an important role in the end of Mark's gospel.[5] Jesus first comes to the temple after his triumphal entry, and after looking around at everything in it, he leaves (11:11). Many interpreters agree that Jesus subsequently prophesies the temple's destruction when he curses the fig tree (11:12–14).[6] Jesus then goes into the temple. He drives out those buying and selling, turns over the tables of the money changers, and speaks out against the corruption of the temple. Many interpreters see Jesus' action as a symbolic act signifying the temple's future cleansing and/or destruction.[7] However, the act is understood, it is clearly performed in response to corruption in the temple, and is intended, literally or symbolically, as an attempted restoration. He also speaks out against the temple and its leaders numerous times; condemning its leaders in the parable of the wicked tenant (12:1–12), speaking out against its corrupt practices (12:41–44),[8] and directly foretelling its future destruction (13:1–2; 14:62).[9] Jesus is also falsely accused of claiming he will destroy the temple and build another (14:58). Finally, at Jesus' crucifixion, the temple veil is torn from top to bottom, another event symbolic of the temple's future destruction and the judgment of its corrupt leaders (15:38).[10]

---

5. For a survey of the temple theme in Mark, see Juel, *Messiah and Temple*, 127–39.

6. See Telford, *Barren Temple*, 48–49; Meier, *A Marginal Jew*, 642 n. 32, 887–88; Münderlein, "Die Verfluchung" 103; Böttger, *Der König der Juden*, 76; Evans, *Mark*, 160; Marcus, *Mark 8–16*, 789–90; Moloney, *Mark*, 225–26. For interpreters who do not read this pericope as a prophecy of the temple's destruction, see Collins, *Mark*, 229–32; Pesch, *Markusevangelium*, 2:189–202.

7. For example, see Crossan, *Historical Jesus*, 357–58; Sanders, *Jesus and Judaism*, 75; Fredriksen, "Jesus and the Temple," 298; Evans, *Mark*, 181–82; Marcus, *Mark 8–16*, 789–83; France, *Mark*, 436–38.

8. For discussion on this pericope and its relationship to temple corruption, see Wright, "Widow's Mites" 256–65; Myers, *Binding the Strong Man*, 320–22; Sugirtharajah, "Widow's Mites," 42–43; Horsley, *Whole Story*, 258n7; Evans, *Mark*, 280–85.

9. Some read this statement by Jesus as a promise of judgment against the corrupt temple authorities. For examples, see van Iersel, *Mark*, 450–51; Moloney, *Mark*, 305 n. 147; Evans, *Mark*, 450–51.

10. For such an interpretation of the tearing of the temple veil, see Evans, *Mark*, 508–10; Lohmeyer, *Das Evangelium*, 347; Pesch, *Markusevangelium*, 2:498–99; Juel, *Messiah and Temple*, 137–39; Donahue, *Are You the Christ*, 203; Marcus, *Mark 8–16*, 1066–68.

Therefore, both narratives address religious corruption related to temple worship. In the Elijah-Elisha narrative, that corruption is related to idolatry and the worship of Baal, while in Mark's gospel, the corruption is related to the Jerusalem temple itself, as well as to the activity of its leaders. Both narratives address the eradication of this corruption. In the Elijah-Elisha narrative, the temples of Baal as well as the priests of Baal are utterly destroyed, while in Mark's gospel, the destruction of the corrupt Jerusalem temple and its leaders is repeatedly foretold and alluded to. Finally, both stories have accounts of temple cleansing—the cleansings in the Elijah-Elisha narrative being literal cleansings (cleansings through destruction) and the cleansing in Mark's narrative being symbolic.

Clearly the evidence that Mark's temple motif is literarily dependent on the temple motif of the Elijah-Elisha narrative is not as strong as that of our previous cases. We lack any specific shared narrative details or narrative structure. Our evidence is limited to thematic similarities that are admittedly general in nature. Therefore, we cannot make a strong claim for literary dependence. However, the fact that we have already demonstrated strong examples of Mark's dependence on the Elijah-Elisha narrative, makes our evidence here stronger that it might otherwise be. On their own, these general thematic similarities prove little, but together with the evidence we have already put forward in previous chapters, at the least, they offer a plausible case for literary influence. We suggest that the centrality that the Markan evangelist gives to the corrupt temple at the end of his narrative might be influenced by this similar motif found at the end of the Elijah-Elisha narrative. The extent and nature of this influence is difficult to determine, but that influence exists seems plausible.

THE RESURRECTION NARRATIVE

Of all the resurrection narratives in the canonical gospels, the Markan resurrection narrative is the most distinct and has drawn the greatest speculation from modern interpreters.[11] The lack of resurrection appearances along with the gospel's abrupt ending have caused many interpreters to posit that the gospel, in its current form, is incomplete and that its original ending has been lost.[12] However, many recent interpreters have

---

11. For a survey of scholarship on the ending of Mark's gospel, see Cox, *History and Critique*.

12. For example, see Bultmann, *Synoptic Tradition*, 285; Swete, *Commentary on*

argued that the gospel's ending is entirely appropriate and consistent with the evangelist's literary and theological purposes.[13] However, few interpreters have provided any type of literary precedent or model that might explain Mark's abrupt ending. We suggest that such a model might be found in the Elijah-Elisha narrative.

Interestingly, both the Gospel of Mark and the Elijah-Elisha narrative conclude with a resurrection account. In 2 Kings 13:20-21, Elisha dies and is buried. The narrative then recounts how some people were burying a dead man, when they were surprised by Moabite raiders. They throw the body into the grave of Elisha and presumably flee in fear. The body of the dead man touches the bones of Elisha, and immediately the man comes to life and rises to his feet.

We suggest that this rather abrupt resurrection narrative that closes the Elijah-Elisha narrative, might provide a literary model or influence for Mark's abrupt ending. Both narratives involve people at a tomb or burial sight. In both stories, the peoples' intended mission is interrupted by something startling—Moabite raiders in 2 Kings 13 and an angel in Mark 16. In both stories, the people at the tomb leave it abruptly in fear. Finally, both stories include the resurrection of a dead person.

Again we recognize that the case here for literary dependence is not as strong as previous cases that we have considered. But in light of the strength of our previous cases, the present case is strengthened and should not be dismissed out of hand. Perhaps this final resurrection episode in the Elijah-Elisha narrative may have only played a minor role in the evangelist's composition of the resurrection narrative. It may have simply given the evangelist literary precedence for the abrupt ending of the gospel. While we cannot be certain of literary dependence here, a literary relationship of some nature seems plausible, even if the nature and extent of that relationship is difficult to determine.

Mark, 398-99; Gundry, *Apology*, 1009-12; Evans, *Mark*, 539; France, *Mark*, 682-84; Croy, *Mutilation*, 165.

13. For example, see Collins, *Mark*, 790; Cox, *History and Critique*, 152-57, 203-4, 223-27; Moloney, *Mark*, 348-52; Hooker, *Mark*, 391-94. For an earlier interpreter who reached a similar conclusion, see Creed, "Conclusion of the Gospel," 175-80. Though Joel Marcus leans toward 16:8 as the original ending, he claims that not enough evidence exists to make a strong conclusion; see Marcus, *Mark 8-16*, 1091-96.

CONCLUSION

As we examine Mark's account of Jesus' passion and resurrection, we see that the evangelist's use of the Elijah-Elisha narrative has diminished or at least become less overt. With Peter's triple denial, we have one clear and distinct example of direct Markan imitation of the Elijah-Elisha narrative. In addition to this example, we have two cases in which literary influence between Mark's gospel and the Elijah-Elisha narrative seems plausible, though the extent nature of the influence is difficult to determine. We suggest two possible reasons for what appears to be the Markan evangelist's diminishing use of the Elijah-Elisha narrative in his passion and resurrection narratives. The first possible reason is that with Jesus' passion and resurrection, the subject matter of Mark's narrative significantly and necessarily diverges in similarity from the subject matter of the Elijah-Elisha narrative. While the ministries of Jesus and those of Elijah and Elisha are able to share many similarities, Jesus' fate is radically different from the fates of Israel's most powerful prophets. The Markan evangelist would therefore be constrained by the historical realities of Jesus' suffering and death and consequently be forced to depart in a significant way from his imitation of the Elijah-Elisha narrative. The second possible reason is the existence of a firmly established passion tradition, a tradition that many gospel interpreters accept. Whether such a tradition existed, and what form it might have existed in is uncertain, but the existence of such a tradition might limit the extent to which the Markan evangelist could incorporate other literary sources.

Conclusions

HERE WE HAVE PROVIDED abundant evidence demonstrating the existence of a significant literary relationship between Mark's gospel and the Elijah-Elisha narrative. We have identified numerous textual markers or clues in Mark's gospel that point the reader to the Elijah-Elisha narrative. In addition to these textual clues, we have provided numerous examples of Mark's direct imitation of the Elijah-Elisha narrative, some of which are clear and obvious, while others are more creative and harder to detect. In light of this evidence, our primary conclusion is that the Elijah-Elisha narrative was an important literary source for the composition of Mark's gospel.

It is important to provide two caveats regarding this primary conclusion. One, we are not claiming that the Elijah-Elisha narrative is the only literary source for Mark's gospel. Clearly there is a significant amount of the gospel that cannot be explained or accounted for by the Elijah-Elisha narrative. It is therefore necessary to continue to look for additional literary sources that the Markan evangelist may have relied on during the composition of the gospel. As Dennis MacDonald suggests, the works of Homer may serve as such a source, though the extent of Mark's use of Homer is uncertain and needs better clarification. While further search for Markan sources in Greco-Roman literature may be helpful, given the evangelist's clear affinity for and obvious use of Jewish Scripture, its exploration is likely to prove more fruitful.

The second caveat regarding our conclusion is that Mark's use of the Elijah-Elisha narrative as a source does not carry with it any implicit conclusions regarding the gospel's meaning or significance. For example, we are not claiming that because Mark has used the Elijah-Elisha narrative as a primary source, that this narrative holds the interpretive key for understanding Mark's gospel. While the significance that Mark's sources have for the interpretation of the gospel may be important, this question is not the subject of the present project, and it will therefore be left for other interpreters to answer. However, we will say that one must be careful in correlating a narrative's source material with a narrative's meaning or significance. At times, an imitating author does not necessarily intend for every aspect of his or her imitation to be detected by the reader, let alone play a role in the reader's construction of meaning. At times, an author might simply desire an imitated text to simply serve as a pattern for constructing a new narrative or perhaps as a quarry from which to draw narrative building blocks. From our analysis of Mark's use of the Elijah-Elisha narrative, it seems that some of Markan imitation is best understood in one of these two ways.

Finally we must note that this project has two significant implications for gospel studies as a whole. First, this project challenges the prevailing standards used in gospels studies for determining literary dependence and therefore, the nature of gospel relationships. It demonstrates that while verbal agreement is a strong piece of evidence for establishing literary dependence, it is not the only useful evidence. By examining the art and technique of Greco-Roman imitation, new ways of establishing literary dependence should be considered by gospel interpreters. Such consideration could have radical implications for our understanding of the canonical gospels' relationship to each other. What have long stood as bedrock conclusions of source and redaction criticism might need to be reconsidered in light of the creative tendencies seen in Greco-Roman imitation. Redactional issues that have long stumped gospel interpreters might find satisfying explanations when Greco-Roman imitation is considered. The relationship between John's gospel and the Synoptics might also be reconsidered.

Second, this project proposes a new way in which gospel writers could use Jewish Scriptures. In addition to using quotations, allusions, and echoes of Jewish Scripture, gospel writers could actually use the very structure, details, and literary formulas found in the narratives of Jewish Scripture to formulate their own narrative traditions. Acknowledging such a use of scripture raises many significant questions. In what ways might such imitation or re-writing of scripture influence a gospel's meaning or significance? In what ways does such use of Jewish Scripture impact the gospel's relationship to history or the search for the historical Jesus? What authority or privilege did the gospel writers attribute to their own work? These and many more questions are raised when we consider the gospel writers imitation of Jewish Scriptures.

Conclusions

Narrowly speaking, this project is an initial step in a renewed search for Markan literary source material. It has identified one significant source for Mark's gospel—the Elijah-Elisha narrative—and calls Markan interpreters to search for additional sources. Broadly speaking, this project, through its specific focus on Markan sources, is a challenge to the status quo in gospels scholarship. It draws attention to a ubiquitous practice in Greco-Roman writing that has long been ignored by gospel interpreters and demonstrates the ramifications that practice has for gospel scholarship.

Bibliography

ANCIENT SOURCES: TEXTS, EDITIONS, TRANSLATIONS

Aristotle. *Physics*. Translated by F. M. Cornford and P. H. Wicksteed. 2 vols. Loeb Classical Library 228 and 255. Cambridge: Harvard University Press, 1934, 1986.

Cicero. *On the Orator*. Translated by E. W. Sutton and H. Rackham. 2 vols. Loeb Classical Library 348-49. Cambridge: Harvard University Press, 1942.

Homer. *Iliad and Odyssey*. Translated by W. F. Wyatt and A. T. Murray. 4 vols. Loeb Classical Library 104-5 and 170-71. Cambridge: Harvard University Press, 1995 and 1999.

Isocrates. Translated by G. Norlin and L. R. van Hook. 3 vols. Loeb Classical Library 209, 229, and 373. Cambridge: Harvard University Press, 1928-1929, 1945.

Novum Testamentum Graece. Edited by E. Nestle and K. Aland. 27th ed. Stuttgart: Deutsche Bibelstiftung, 1993.

Plato. *Republic*. Translated by P. Shorey. 2 vols. Loeb Classical Library 237 and 276. Cambridge: Harvard University Press, 1930, 1935.

Propertius Elegies. Translated by G. P. Goold. Loeb Classical Library 18. Cambridge: Harvard University Press, 1990.

Quintillian. *The Orator's Education*. Translated by D. A. Russell. 5 vols. Loeb Classical Library 124-27 and 494. Cambridge: Harvard University Press, 2002.

Septuagint, id est, Vetus Testamentum Graece iuxta LXX interpretes. Edited by A. Rahlfs. 2 vols. 8th ed. Stuttgart: Württembergishe Bibelanstalt, 1965.

Virgil. *Aeneid*. Translated by H. R. Fairclough. 2 vols. Loeb Classical Library 63-64. Cambridge: Harvard University Press, 1999.

SECONDARY LITERATURE

Aune, D. E. *The New Testament in its Literary Environment*. Library of Early Christianity 8. Philadelphia: Westminster, 1987.

Aus, R. D. *The Wicked Tenants and Gethsemane: Isaiah in the Wicked Tenants Vineyard, and Moses and the High Priest in Gethsemane: Judaic Traditions in Mark 12:1-9 and 14:32-42*. University of South Florida International Studies in Formative Christianity and Judaism 4. Atlanta: Scholars, 1996.

Barrett, C. K. *The Gospel according to St. John: An Introduction with Commentary and Notes on the Greek Text*. 2nd ed. Philadelphia: Westminster, 1978.

Baumgarten, J. M. "4Q500 and the Ancient Conception of the Lord's Vineyard." *Journal of Jewish Studies* 40 (1989) 1-6.

Beasley-Murray, G. R. *John*. Word Biblical Commentary 36. Waco, TX: Word, 1987.

Bibliography

Black, C. C. "The Quest of the Markan Redactor: Why Has It Been Pursued and What Has It Taught Us?" *Journal for the Study of the New Testament* 33 (1988) 19–39.

———. *The Disciples according to Mark: Markan Redaction in Current Debate*. Journal for the Study of the New Testament: Supplemental Series 27. Sheffield: JSOT Press, 1989.

Black, M. "The Christological Use of the Old Testament in the New Testament." *New Testament Studies* 18 (1971–72) 1–14.

Blomberg, C. L. "Form Criticism." Pages 444–50 in *Dictionary of Jesus and the Gospels*. Edited by J. B. Green et al. Downers Grove, IL: IVP, 1992.

Bonner, S. F. *Education in Ancient Rome: From the Elder Cato to the Younger Pliny*. Berkeley: University of California Press, 1977.

Boring, M. E. *Mark: A Commentary*. New Testament Library. Louisville: Westminster John Knox, 2006.

Böttger, P. C. *Der König der Juden—das Heil für die Völker*. Neukirchen Studienbücher 13. Neukirchen: Neukirchener, 1981.

Branscomb, B. H. *The Gospel of Mark*. Moffatt New Testament Commentary 2. London: Hodder & Stoughton, 1937.

Brodie, T. L. *The Crucial Bridge: The Elijah-Elisha Narrative as an Interpretive Synthesis of Genesis-Kings and a Literary Model for the Gospels*. Collegeville, MN: Liturgical, 2000.

———. *The Birthing of the New Testament: Intertextual Development of the New Testament Writings*. New Testament Monographs 1. Sheffield: Sheffield Phoenix, 2004.

Brooke, G. J. "4Q500 1 and the Use of Scripture in the Parable of the Vineyard." *Dead Sea Discoveries* 2 (1995) 268–94.

Brown, R. E. *The Gospel according to John I–XII: A New Translation with Introduction and Commentary*. Anchor Bible 29. Garden City, NY: Doubleday, 1966.

———. "Jesus and Elisha." *Perspectives* 12 (1971) 85–104.

———. *The Death of the Messiah: From Gethsemane to the Grave: A Commentary on the Passion Narratives in the Four Gospels*. Anchor Bible Reference Library. 2 vols. New York: Doubleday, 1994.

Bultmann, R. *The History of the Synoptic Tradition*. Translated by John Marsh. Oxford: Blackwell, 1963 (1921).

———. *Theology of the New Testament*. 2 vols. Translated by Kendrick Grobel. New York: Scribner, 1951–55.

Burridge, R. *What Are the Gospels? A Comparison with Graeco-Roman Biography*. 2nd rev. ed. Grand Rapids: Eerdmans, 2004.

Carlston, C. E. *The Parables of the Triple Tradition*. Philadelphia: Fortress, 1975.

Collins, A. Yarbro. *Mark: A Commentary*. Hermeneia. Minneapolis: Fortress, 2007.

Conroy, C. "Hiel between Ahab and Elijah-Elisha: 1 Kings 6,34 in Its Immediate Context." *Biblica* 77 (1996) 210–18.

Corley, K. E. *Private Woman, Public Meals: Social Conflict in the Synoptic Tradition*. Peabody, MA: Hendrickson, 1993.

Cox, S. L. *A History and Critique of Scholarship concerning the Markan Ending*. Lewiston, NY: Edwin Mellen, 1993.

Cranfield, C. E. B. *The Gospel According to St. Mark*. Cambridge Greek Testament Commentary. Cambridge: Cambridge University Press, 1959.

Creed, J. M. "The Conclusion of the Gospel according to Saint Mark." *Journal of Theological Studies* 31 (1930) 175–80.

Bibliography

Crossan, J. D. *The Historical Jesus: The Life of a Mediterranean Jewish Peasant*. San Francisco: HarperSanFrancisco, 1991.

Croy, N. C. *The Mutilation of Mark's Gospel*. Nashville: Abingdon, 2003.

Dautzenberg, G. "Elija im Markusevangelium." Pages 1077-94 in vol. 2 *The Four Gospels 2. Festschrift for F. Neirynck*. Edited by F. Van Segbroek, et al. 3 vols. Bibliotheca Ephemeridum Theologicarum Lovaniensium 100. Leuven: Leuven University/ Peeters, 1992.

Dewey, K. E. "Peter's Curse and Cursed Peter." Pages 96-114 in *The Passion in Mark*. Edited by Werner Kelber. Philadelphia: Fortress, 1976.

Dibelius, M. *From Tradition to Gospel*. Translated by Bertram Lee Woolf. Cambridge: James Clarke, 1971 (1934).

Dodd, C. H. *Historical Tradition in the Fourth Gospel*. New Edition. Cambridge: Cambridge University Press, 1976.

Donahue, J. R. *Are You the Christ: The Trial Narrative in the Gospel of Mark*. Society of Biblical Literature Dissertation Series 10. Missoula: Scholars, 1973.

Donahue, J. R., and Daniel J. Harrington. *The Gospel of Mark*. Sacra Pagina 2. Collegeville, MN: Liturgical, 2002.

Dormeyer, D. *Das Markusevangelium als Idealbiographie von Jesus Christus, dem Nazarener*. Stuttgarter biblische Beiträge 43. Stuttgart: Katholisches Bibelwerk, 1999.

Dowd, S. E. Review of Dennis MacDonald, *The Homeric Epics and the Gospel of Mark*. *Catholic Biblical Quarterly* 63 (2001) 155-56.

Dunn, J. D. G. *Christianity in the Making: Jesus Remembered*. Grand Rapids: Eerdmans, 2003.

Ernst, J. *Das Evangelium nach Markus*. Regensburger Neues Testament 2. Regensburg: Pustet, 1998.

Evans, C. A. "On the Vineyard Parables of Isaiah 5 and Mark 12." *Biblische Zeitschrift* 28 (1984) 82-86.

―――. "Did Jesus Predict His Death and Resurrection." Pages 82-97 in *Resurrection*. Edited by Stanley E. Porter et al. Journal for the Study of the New Testament Supplemental Series 186. Sheffield: Sheffield Academic, 1999.

―――. *Mark 8:27—16:20*. Word Biblical Commentary 34b. Nashville: Nelson, 2001.

―――. "The Beginning of the Good News and the Fulfillment of Scripture in Mark's Gospel." Pages 83-103 in *Hearing the Old Testament in the New Testament*. Edited by Stanley E. Porter. Grand Rapids: Eerdmans, 2006.

Farrell, J. "The Virgilian Intertext." Pages 223-38 in *The Cambridge Companion to Virgil*. Edited by Charles Martindale. Cambridge: Cambridge University Press, 1997.

Feine, P. *Eine vorkanonische Überlieferung des Lukas im Evangelium und Apostelgeschichte*. Gotha: Perthes, 1891.

―――. *Einleitung in das Neue Testament*. 3rd ed. Leipzig: Quelle & Meyer, 1923.

Fiske, G. C. *Lucilius and Horace: A Study in the Classical Theory of Imitation*. Westport, CT: Greenwood, 1920.

France, R. T. *The Gospel of Mark*. New International Greek Testament Commentary. Grand Rapids: Eerdmans, 2002.

Fredriksen, P. "Jesus and the Temple, Mark and the War." Pages 293-310 in *SBL 1990 Seminar Papers*. Edited by D. J. Lull. Atlanta: Scholars, 1990.

Gilmour, M. Review of Dennis MacDonald, *The Homeric Epics and the Gospel of Mark*. *Review of Biblical Literature* 9 (2002). http://www.bookreviews.org/pdf/931_2905 .pdf.

Bibliography

Gnilka, J. *Das Evangelium nach Markus*. 2 vols. Evangelisch-katholischer Kommentar zum Neuen Testament 2. Zurich: Neukirchener, 1979.

Guelich, R. *Mark 1—8:26*. Word Biblical Commentary 34A. Dallas: Word, 1989.

Guillaume, P. "Miracles Miraculously Repeated: Gospel Miracles as Duplication of Elijah-Elisha's." *Biblische Notizen* 98 (1999) 21-23.

Gundry, R. *Mark: A Commentary on His Apology for the Cross*. Grand Rapids: Eerdmans, 1993.

Haenchen, E. *John 1*. Hermeneia. Philadelphia: Fortress, 1980.

Hardie, C. G. "Virgil." Pages 1123-28 in the *Oxford Classical Dictionary*. 2nd ed. Edited by N. G. L. Hammond and H. H. Scullard. Oxford: Oxford University Press, 1970.

Hauser, A. J., and R. Gregory. *From Carmel to Horeb: Elijah in Crisis*. Bible and Literature 19. Sheffield: Almond, 1990.

Hock, R. F. Review of Dennis R. MacDonald, *The Homeric Epics and the Gospel of Mark*. *Review of Biblical Literature* 4 (2002) 363-67.

Holtzmann, H. *Die synoptischen Evangelien: Ihr Ursprung und geschichtlicher Character*. Leipzig: Wilhelm Engelmann, 1863.

Hooker, M. *The Gospel According to St. Mark*. Blacks New Testament Commentaries. Peabody: Hendrickson, 1991.

———. Review of Dennis R. MacDonald, *The Homeric Epics and the Gospel of Mark*. *Journal of Theological Studies* 53 (2002) 196-98.

Horsley, R. A. *Hearing the Whole Story: The Politics of Plot in Mark's Gospel*. Louisville: Westminster John Knox, 2001.

Iersel, B. M. F., van. *Mark: A Reader Response Commentary*. Journal for the Study of the New Testament Supplement Series 164. Sheffield: Sheffield Academic, 1998.

Incigneri, B. J. *The Gospel to the Romans: The Setting and Rhetoric of Mark's Gospel*. Leiden: Brill, 2003.

Jeremias, J. *The Parables of Jesus*. Rev. ed. New York: Scribner, 1963.

Juel, D. *Messiah and Temple: The Trial of Jesus in the Gospel of Mark*. Society of Biblical Literature Dissertation Series 31. Missoula: Scholars, 1977.

Kahler, Martin. *The So-called Historical Jesus and the Historic, Biblical Christ*. Translated and edited by Carl Braaten. Philadelphia: Fortress, 1964.

Käsemann, E. "The Problem of the Historical Jesus." Pages 15-47 in *Essays on New Testament Themes*. Studies in Biblical Theology 41. London: SCM, 1964.

Kelber, W. H. *The Kingdom in Mark: A New Place and New Time*. Philadelphia: Fortress, 1974.

Klein, G. "Die Verleugnung des Petrus." *Zeitschrift für Theologie und Kirche* 58 (1961) 285-328.

Klostermann, E. *Das Markusevangelium*. 4th ed. Handbuch zum Neuen Testament 3. Tübingen: Mohr/Siebeck, 1950.

Knauer, G. N. *Die Aeneis und Homer: Studien zur poetischen Technik Vergils mit Listen der Homerzitate in der Aeneis*. Hypomnemata 7. Göttingen: Vandenhoeck & Ruprecht, 1964.

———. "Vergil and Homer." *ANRW* 31.2, 871-914. Edited by H. Temporini and W. Haase. Berlin: de Gruyter, 1980.

Leo, F. *Die griechisch-römische Biographie nach ihrer literarischen Form*. Leipzig: Teubner, 1901.

Lindars, B. "Elijah, Elisha and the Gospel Miracles." Pages 63-79 in *Miracles*. Edited by C. F. D. Moule. London: Mowbray, 1965.

Bibliography

Lightfoot, R. H. *Locality and Doctrine in the Gospels.* New York: Harper, 1938.

Lohmeyer, E. *Galiläa und Jerusalem.* Forschungen zur Religion und Literatur des Alten und Neuen Testaments 52. Gottingen: Vandenhoeck & Ruprecht, 1936.

———. "Das Gleichnis von den bösen Weingärtnern (Mark 12,1–12)." *Zeitschrift für systematische Theologie* 18 (1941) 242–59.

———. *Das Evangelium des Markus.* 15th ed. Kritisch-exegetischer Kommentar über das Neue Testament. Göttingen: Vandenhoeck & Ruprecht, 1959.

———. *Lord of the Temple: A Study of the Relation between Cult and Gospel.* Edinburgh: Oliver & Boyd, 1961.

Lührmann, D. *Das Markusevangelium.* Tübingen: Mohr/Siebeck, 1987.

MacDonald, D. *Christianizing Homer: "The Odyssey," Plato, and "The Acts of Andrew."* New York: Oxford University Press, 1994.

———. *The Homeric Epics and the Gospel of Mark.* New Haven: Yale University Press, 2000.

Mahnke, H. *Die Versuchungsgeschichte im Rahmen der synoptischen Evangelien. Ein Beitrag zur frühen Christologie.* Beiträge zur biblischen Exegese Theologie 9. Frankfurt: Lang, 1978.

Mann, C. S. *Mark.* Anchor Bible 27. Garden City, NY: Doubleday, 1986.

Marcus, J. *The Way of the Lord: Christological Exegesis of the Old Testament in the Gospel of Mark.* Edinburgh: T. & T. Clark, 1992.

———. *Mark 1–8: A New Translation with Introduction and Commentary.* Anchor Bible 27. New York: Doubleday, 2000.

———. *Mark 8–16: A New Translation with Introduction and Commentary.* Anchor Bible 27A. New Haven: Yale University Press, 2009.

Marrou, H. I. *A History of Education in Antiquity.* Translated by George Lamb. New York: Sheed & Ward, 1956.

Marxsen, W. *Mark the Evangelist.* Translated by James Boyce et al. Nashville: Abingdon, 1969.

Masson, C. "Le reniement de Pierre. Quelques aspects de la formation d'une tradition." *Revue D'Historie et de Philosophie Religieuses* 37 (1957) 24–35.

McKeon, R. "Literary Criticism and the Concept of Imitation in Antiquity." *Modern Philology* 34 (1936) 1–35.

Meier, J. P. *A Marginal Jew: Mentor Message and Miracles.* Vol. 2. New York: Doubleday, 1994.

———. *A Marginal Jew: Companions and Competitors.* Vol. 3. New York: Doubleday, 2001.

Mell, U. *Die "anderen" Winzer: Eine exegetische Studie zur Vollmacht Jesu Christi nach Markus 11,27—12,34.* Wissenschaftliche Untersuchungen zum Neuen Testament 77. Tübingen: Mohr/Siebeck, 1995.

Miller, D., and P. Miller. *The Gospel of Mark as Midrash on Earlier Jewish and New Testament Literature.* Lewiston, NY: Mellen, 1990.

Moffatt, J. *An Introduction to the Literature of the New Testament.* 3rd ed. Edinburgh: T. & T. Clark, 1918.

Moloney, F. J. "The End of the Son of Man?" *Downside Review* 98 (1980) 280–90.

———. "The Fourth Gospel and the Jesus of History." *New Testament Studies* 46 (2000) 42–58.

———. *The Gospel of Mark: A Commentary.* Peabody, MA: Hendrickson, 2002.

Bibliography

Momigliano, A. *The Development of Greek Biography*. Cambridge: Harvard University Press, 1971.
Morgenthaler, R. *Statistik des neutestamentlichen Wortschatzes*. Zurich: Gotthelf, 1958.
Morris, L. *The Gospel according to John*. Rev. ed. New International Commentary on the New Testament. Grand Rapids: Eerdmans, 1995.
Münderlein, G. "Die Verfluchung des Feigenbaumes (Mk XI 12–14)." *New Testament Studies* 10 (1963) 89–104.
Myers, C. *Binding the Strong Man: A Political Reading of Mark's Story of Jesus*. Maryknoll, NY: Orbis, 1988.
Nelis, D. *Vergil's Aeneid and the Argonautica of Apollonius Rhodius*. ARCA 39. Leeds; Francis Carins, 2001.
Nineham, D. E. *The Gospel of St. Mark*. New York: Seabury, 1968.
Nolland, J. Review of Dennis R. MacDonald, *The Homeric Epics and the Gospel of Mark*. *Anvil* 18 (2001), 134–35.
O'Leary, A. M. *Matthew's Judaization of Mark: Examined in the Context of the Use of Sources in Graeco-Roman Antiquity*. Library of New Testament Studies 323. London: T. & T. Clark, 2006.
O'Toole, R. F. "Last Supper." Pages 237–39 in *Anchor Bible Dictionary*. Volume 4. Edited by D. N. Freedman. Doubleday: New York, 1992.
Pagliara, C. *La figura di Elia nel Vangelo di Marco: Aspetti semantici e funzionali*. Rome: Editrice Pontificia Università Gregoriana, 2003.
Perrin, N. "Towards an Interpretation of the Gospel of Mark." Pages 10–21 in *Christology and a Modern Pilgrimage: A Discussion with Norman Perrin*. Edited by H. D. Betz. Claremont: SBL, 1974.
Pesch, R. *Das Markusevangelium*. 2 vols. Herders theologischer Kommentar zum Neuen Testament 2. Freiburg: Herder, 1976.
———. *Naherwartungen: Tradition und Redaktion in Mark 13*. Kommentare und Beiträge zum Alten und Neuen Testament. Düsseldorf: Patmos, 1968.
Quesnell, Q. *The Mind of Mark: Interpretation and Method through the Exegesis of Mark 6,52*. Rome: Pontifical Biblical Institute Press, 1969.
Robbins, V. "Form Criticism: New Testament." Pages 841–44 in *Anchor Bible Dictionary*. Volume 4. Edited by D. N. Freedman. New York: Doubleday, 1992.
Roth, W. *Hebrew Gospel: Cracking the Code of Mark*. Oak Park, IL: Meyer-Stone, 1988.
Sahlin, H. *Der Messias und das Gottesfolk; Studien zur protolukanischen Theologie*. Acta Seminarii Neotestamentici Upsaliensis 12. Uppsala: Almqvist & Wiksell, 1945.
Sanders, E. P. *Jesus and Judaism*. Philadelphia: Fortress, 1985.
———. *The Historical Figure of Jesus*. London: Penguin, 1993.
Sandnes, K. O. "*Imitatio Homeri*? An Appraisal of Dennis R. MacDonald's 'Mimesis Criticism.'" *Journal of Biblical Literature* 124 (2005) 715–32.
Schille, G. "Die Seesturmerzählungen Markus 4,35–51 als Beispiel neutestamentlicher Actualisierung." *Zeitschrift für neutestamentliche Wissenschaft* 56 (1965) 30–40.
Schmid, J. *The Gospel according to Mark*. Regensburg New Testament. Staten Island, NY: Alba House, 1968.
Schnackenburg, R. *The Gospel According to St. John*. 3 vols. Translated by Kevin Smyth. Herders theologischer Kommentar zum Neuen Testament 4. London: Burns & Oates, 1982.
Stein, R. H. *Mark*. Baker Exegetical Commentary on the New Testament. Grand Rapids: Baker, 2008.

Bibliography

———. "Last Supper." Pages 444–50 in *Dictionary of Jesus and the Gospels*. Edited by J. B. Green, et al. Downers Grove, IL: IVP, 1992.

Stern, D. *Parables in Midrash: Narrative and Exegesis in Rabbinic Literarture*. Cambridge: Harvard University Press, 1991.

Streeter, B. H. *The Four Gospels: A Study of Origins*. London: Macmillan, 1924.

Sugirtharajah, R. S. "The Widow's Mites Revalued." *Expository Times* 103 (1991–92) 42–43.

Swete, H. B. *Commentary on Mark: The Greek Text with Introduction, Notes and Indexes*. Grand Rapids: Kregel, 1977 (1898).

Talbert, C. H. *What Is a Gospel? The Genre of the Canonical Gospels*. Philadelphia: Fortress, 1977.

Taylor, V. *Behind the Third Gospel: A Study of the Proto-Lukan Hypothesis*. Oxford: Oxford University Press, 1926.

———. *The Formation of the Gospel Tradition: Eight Lectures*. London: MacMillan, 1933.

Telford, W. R. *The Barren Temple and the Withered Tree. A Redaction-critical Analysis of the Cursing of the Fig Tree Pericope in Mark's Gospel and Its Relationship to the Cleansing of the Temple Tradition*. Journal for the Study of the New Testament Supplement Series 1. Sheffield: Sheffield Academic, 1980.

Theissen, G. *The Miracle Stories of the Early Christian Tradition*. Translated by F. McDonagh. Edited by J. Riches. Edinburgh: T. & T. Clark, 1983.

———. *The Gospels in Context: Social and Political History in the Synoptic Tradition*. Translated by Linda Maloney. Minneapolis: Fortress, 1991.

Trible, P. "Exegesis for Storytellers and Other Strangers." *Journal of Biblical Literature* 114 (1995) 3–19.

Votaw, C. "The Gospels and Contemporary Biographies." *American Journal of Theology* 19 (1915) 45–73, 217–49.

Walsh, P. G. *Livy: His Historical Aims and Methods*. Cambridge: Cambridge University Press, 1961.

Watts, R. *Isaiah's New Exodus in Mark*. Wissenschaftliche Untersuchungen zum Neuen Testament 2/88. Tübingen: Mohr/Siebeck, 1997.

Weeden, T. J. *Mark-Traditions in Conflict*. Philadelphia: Fortress, 1971.

Weiss, J. *Das älteste Evangelium: Ein Eitrag zum Verständnis des Markus-Evangeliums und der ältesten evangelischen Überlieferung*. Göttingen: Vandenhoeck & Ruprecht, 1903.

Weizsacker, C. *Untersuchungen über die evangelische Geschichte*. 2nd ed. Tübingen: Mohr/Siebeck, 1901.

Weren, W. J. C. "The Use of Isaiah 5,1–7 in the Parable of the Tentants (Mark 12,1–12; Matthew 21,33–46)." *Biblica* 79 (1998) 1–26.

Winn, A. *The Purpose of Mark's Gospel: An Early Christian Response to Roman Imperial Propaganda*. Wissenschaftliche Untersuchungen zum Neuen Testament 2/245. Tübingen: Mohr/Siebeck, 2008.

Wright, A. G. "The Widow's Mites: Praise of Lament?—A Matter of Context." *Catholic Biblical Quarterly* 44 (1982) 256–65.

Subject Index

Aeneas, 13–31
Aeneid, 9–14, 23–24, 28–29, 34–35
Ahab, 10, 53, 67, 102–6, 108, 112

Biography, 62–66

Conflation, 23, 29, 73

Diffusion, 30, 97–98

Elijah 10, 51–84, 88–90, 92–102, 105, 108–14, 115–19
Elisha 10, 51–84, 88–90, 92–102, 105, 108–14, 115–19

Form Criticism, 2–4, 7, 62

Genre, 37, 61–66

Healing, 3, 51, 54–55, 67, 77–81, 85, 90, 94, 98
Historiography, 62–66
Homer/Homeric, 1, 8–12, 14, 16–44, 46, 48–49, 69, 72, 117

Iliad, 9–13, 23–24, 29, 34–35
Imitation, 8–10, 12, 14, 16–17, 19–37, 39–44, 46–50, 55, 59, 69–73, 75, 79–84, 88–94, 97, 99, 107–9, 112, 116–18
Imitative Techniques, 29, 78, 90, 108,
Intensification, 17, 24, 30, 74–75, 78, 83

Jehu, 71, 73, 76, 102, 104–8, 112

Jerusalem, 35, 45, 47, 67–68, 93, 96–97, 99, 103, 112–14
Jezebel, 52, 72, 102, 105, 108, 112
John the Baptist, 51–53, 56, 67, 69–71, 76, 79, 103

Leper/Leprosy, 51, 55, 58, 77–79, 90
Literary Sources, 1–3, 7–9, 37, 69, 116–17

Mimesis, 8–10, 34, 37

Naboth, 54–55, 59, 102–3, 105

Odysseus /Odyssean, 13–23, 25–30, 32, 35–36, 40–45, 47–49
Odyssey, 9–15, 18, 25, 28–29, 32, 34–35, 40, 44–45, 48,
Omission, 30, 78, 80

Passion Prediction, 92–96, 98–99
Peter, 53, 74–75, 92, 98, 110–12, 116

Redaction Criticism, 2–3, 7, 37, 118
Resurrection, 62, 94, 109, 114–16
Reversal, 13–14, 17, 20, 23, 25, 29, 70, 79–81, 97, 107, 112

Source Criticism, 2–3, 7

Temple, 17–19, 22, 45, 48, 52–54, 63, 68, 78, 103, 105–7, 112–14

Virgil/Virgilian, 9–35, 49, 72–73, 75, 78, 80, 91, 97

Author Index

Aune, D. E., 51, 62, 66
Aus, R. D., 100

Barrett, C. K., 4
Baumgarten, J. M., 100
Beasley-Murray, G., 4
Black, C. C., 110
Black, M., 100
Blomberg, C. L., 2
Bonner, S. F., 34
Boring, M. E., 57, 92, 100, 103
Böttger, P. C., 113
Branscomb, B. H., 93
Brodie, T. L., ix, 1–2, 7, 8, 10, 61, 64, 74, 77
Brooke, G. J., 100, 103
Brown, R. E., 4, 51, 93, 110
Bultmann, R., 2, 61, 93, 110, 114
Burridge, R. 62, 64–65

Carlston, C. E., 100
Collins, A. Y., 42, 51, 62–63, 65, 69–70, 74–75, 92–95, 100–101, 103, 113, 115
Conroy, C., 10
Corley, K. E., 89
Cox, S. L., 114, 115
Cranfield, C. E. B., 85
Creed, J. M., 115
Crossan, J. D., 113
Croy, N. C., 115

Dautzenberg, G., 51
Dewey, K. E., 110
Dibelius, M., 2, 61, 93, 110

Dodd, C. H., 4
Donahue, J. R., 57, 71, 82, 103–4, 113
Dormeyer, D., 62
Dowd, S. E., 36
Dunn, J. D. G., 67, 110

Ernst, J., 83
Evans, C. A., 62, 93, 100–101, 103–4, 110, 113, 115

Farrell, J., 11
Feine, P., 2
Fiske, G., 32
France, R. T., 57, 70–71, 82, 92, 100, 104, 113, 115
Fredriksen, P., 113

Gilmour, M., 36
Gnilka, J., 100
Gregory, R., 10
Guelich, R., 1, 42, 57
Guillaume, P., 51
Gundry, R., 42, 82, 103, 115

Haenchen, E., 4
Hardie, C. G., 11–12
Harrington, D., 57, 71, 82, 103–4
Hauser, A. J., 10
Hock, R. F., 36
Holtzmann, H., 2
Hooker, M., 36, 42, 57, 82, 89, 92–93, 100, 115
Horsley, R. A., 113

Author Index

Iersel, B. M. F., van, 42, 51, 57, 70–71, 74, 82, 92, 103, 113
Incigneri, B. J., 62
Jeremias, J., 100
Juel, D., 113

Kahler, M., 109
Käsemann, E., 93
Kelber, W. H., 67
Klein, G., 110
Klostermann, E., 100
Knauer, G. N., 11

Leo, F., 62
Lightfoot, R. H., 67
Lindars, B., 51
Lohmeyer, E., 67, 100, 103, 113
Lührmann, D., 85, 104

MacDonald, D. R., 1, 8–9, 34–47, 49–50, 69, 82, 117
Mahnke, H., 72–73
Mann, C. S., 1
Marcus, J., 1, 51, 70–71, 74, 82–83, 89, 92, 100–101, 103, 113, 115
Marrou, H. I., 34
Marxsen, W., 67
Masson, C., 110
McKeon, R., 8
Meier, J. P., 110, 113
Mell, U., 101
Miller, D., 51
Miller, P., 51
Moffatt, J., 2
Moloney, F. J., 57–58, 67, 82, 89, 92–94, 100, 103–4, 113, 115
Momigliano, A., 62
Morgenthaler, R., 64–65
Morris, L., 4
Münderlein, G., 113
Myers, C., 113

Nelis, D., 9
Nineham, D. E., 85, 93

Nolland, J., 36

O'Leary, A. M., 8
O'Toole, R. F., 7

Pagliara, C., 51
Perrin, N., 93–94
Pesch, R., 57, 82, 92, 100, 113

Quesnell, Q., 83

Robbins, V., 2
Roth, W., 2, 51–60, 79–80, 84

Sahlin, H., 2
Sanders, E. P., 110, 113
Sandnes, K. O., 36, 39, 69, 70
Schille, G., 42
Schmid, J., 61, 100
Schnackenburg, R., 4
Stein, R. H., 7, 57
Stern, D., 103
Streeter, B. H., 2
Sugirtharajah, R. S., 113
Swete, H. B., 114

Talbert, C. H., 62
Taylor, V., 2, 110
Telford, W. R., 6
Theissen, G., 42, 67, 85
Trible, P., 10

Votaw, C., 62

Walsh, P. G., 72–73
Watts, R., 70
Weeden, T. J., 67
Weiss, J., 62, 110
Weizsacker, C., 2
Weren, W. J. C., 100
Winn, A., 62, 98
Wright, A. G., 113

Ancient Literature Index

OLD TESTAMENT

Exodus
4:6–7	77
23:20	69

Leviticus
13–14	77

Numbers
12:10–15	77

Deuteronomy
24:8	77

2 Samuel
3:29	77
14:33	58

1 Kings
13:2	52
16:31–34	105
17:4–7	73
17:7–16	84, 86–89
17:17–24	57, 85
18:3–5	105
18:4	52
19:1–7	54
19	73
19:1–3	105
19:4	72
19:4–9	71
19:4–21	71, 75–76
19:18	54
19:19–21	74
20:39–43	105
21	105

2 Kings
1:3	81
1:1–17	80
1:4, 6	79
1:8	71
1:16	79
2	94–97, 99, 110
2:1–12	53, 98–99
2:2	11
2:3–4	96
2:4, 6	94, 111
2:8	57
2:9–11	97
2:10	95–96
4:7	54
4:42–44	82–84
4:43	52
5:1–19	77–78
5:5–6	96
5:5, 9	77
5:11	78–79
5:14	78
5:20–27	77
5:22	54
7:3–10	77
7:3–16	57
8:13	54
8:16–29	65
9	100, 103–4, 107–8
9:14–26	106–7
11:17–18	54
13:1–13	65

Ancient Literature Index

13:20–21	115	1:16–20	58, 74
15:5	77	1:40	77
		1:41	78
2 Chronicles		1:42	78
26:16–21	77	1:40–45	77–78
		2:1–12	77, 80
Psalms		2:7	80
80:8	103	3:19–30	80
106:23–32	42	4:35–41	40, 44
107:23–32	42	6:8–9	54
		6:15	57
Isaiah		6:30–44	77, 82–83
5:1–7	100–101, 108	7:24–30	54, 77, 84, 86–87, 89
5:2	101	7:31–37	85
27:2–6	103	7:37	52, 57
40:3	69	8:1–10	77, 82–83
		8:27—10:45	98–99, 109
Jeremiah		8:28	57
2:21	103	8:31	94, 96
12:10	103	8:34–38	75
		9:4–5	92
Malachi		9:7	103
3:1	69–70	9:9–13	71
3:22	70	9:11–13	93
3:23–24	69	9:13	56
		9:30—10:31	96
NEW TESTAMENT		10:21	54
Matthew		10:28–31	75
8:5–13	3	10:32–40	97
10:8	77	10:32–34	94
26:26–29	4–6	10:38	95
		10:40	96
Mark		11:1–14	44–45
1:1	103	11:11	113
1:1–13	57	11:12–14	113
1:2–3	69	11:27	103
1:6	71	11:27–33	52
1:11	103	12:1	101
1:12–13	54	12:1–12	100, 106–7, 113
1:12–20	71, 75–76	12:12	103
1:13	73	12:41–44	113
1:14–15	73	13:1–2	113
		14:22–25	4–6
		14:3–9	45

Ancient Literature Index

14:31	111
14:58	113
14:62	113
14:66–72	53
15:34–36	109
15:38	113
16:1–8	58

Luke

7:1–10	3
11:5	77
22:15–20	4–6

John

4:46–54	3

1 Corinthians

11:23–25	4–6

OLD TESTAMENT APOCRYPHA/ PSEUDEPIGRAPHA AND DEAD SEA SCROLLS

1 Enoch

89:56	103
89:66–67	103

Dead Sea Scrolls

4Q500	103

ANCIENT GREEK AND ROMAN AUTHORS

Aristotle
Physis

2.2.194a22	8
2.8.199a15–17	8

Cicero
On the Orator

2.21.90	8

Homer
Iliad

23.257–895	23
23.664–99	26

Odyssey

6–7	44–45
10.1–69	40, 44
10.133–73	14, 16
10–11	28
12.260–450	14, 16
12.317–18	17

Isocrates
Against the Sophists

17–18	8

Panegyrics

10	8

Quintillian
Institutes of Oratory

10.1.19–20	8

Plato
Republic

3.392D–394C	8
4.500C–E	8

Virgil
Aeneid

1.157–560	16
1.166–69	17
5.362–484	26
5.827–71	28–29
6.156–235	28–29
6.337–83	28–29
7.1–7	28–29

www.ingramcontent.com/pod-product-compliance
Lightning Source LLC
Chambersburg PA
CBHW070917160426
43193CB00011B/1498